Storytelling in Therapy

Storytelling in Therapy

Rhiannon Crawford

Brian Brown

Paul Crawford

Published in 2004 by:
Nelson Thornes Ltd
Delta Place
27 Bath Road
CHELTENHAM
GL53 7TH
United Kingdom

04 05 06 07 08 / 10 9 8 7 6 5 4 3 2 1

A catalogue record for this book is available from the British Library

ISBN 0 7487 6932 3

Page make-up by Acorn Bookwork Ltd, Salisbury

Printed and bound in Spain by GraphyCems

CONTENTS

DEDICATION

To Ruby with love

1 STORYTELLING IN THERAPY

Telling stories is as much part of us as breathing air or as Wright (1995) puts it: 'We all need stories for our minds as much as we need food for our bodies .... Stories are motivating, rich in language experience, and inexpensive!' (pp. 5–6). There is nothing so magical as a story and storytelling is a major form of human communication that stretches back to the earliest times and continues today in all kinds of ways, whether to teach, inspire, pass on knowledge or ideals, or even to convey how we should behave. There is a wealth of stories available to us, from myths and legends, to tales of heroes, sagas, epics, folk tales, fables, fairy tales and parables. The range of stories is huge and can be found in pictures, film, cartoons, fiction, biography, history and so on. Most commonly, stories are used in our everyday conversations with one another, when we share real life experiences, values and attitudes. We all 'tell tales', 'spin yarns' or profess the equivalent of Max Bygraves's 'I wanna tell you a story' – all of which can be viewed as giving a performance. Furthermore, each of us has access to a rich collection of stories that have been told to us, read from books down the years or invented ourselves. As Teresa Grainger (1997) writes: 'Storytelling is an ancient art form, an integral part of human existence, and the most enduring form of education. It is an accessible and creative form of communicating and reflecting upon experience, both real and imagined ...' (p. 13).

The term 'storytelling' might trick us into thinking that stories are not part of serious communication and merely for entertainment. This is quite wrong. Stories can powerfully communicate what it is like to be in the world and can provide opportunities to change our view of reality. In other words, they can transform our thinking about ourselves in the world. As such they 'belong not to our tradition of print but to speech, not to our skill in reading, but to our natural urge to listen and talk' (Jones & Buttrey, 1970, p. 1).

All of us are storytellers of one kind or another, although often we don't think of ourselves in this way. Teresa Grainger (1997), in accounting for the prominent role of the storyteller in human societies from the earliest times, writes: 'Humans are natural tellers of tales. Friends share anecdotes of everyday living, relatives recall family folklore, and everyone reflects upon the past and anticipates the future in words and thoughts shaped as stories' (p. 146). In terms of therapy, storytelling by the therapist might help clients think and behave in new, productive ways. As Ruth Tooze (1959) commented in her early book on storytelling: '... a good story not only meets you at some point of your experience but makes you want to go on from here to there, often equipping you for the going. It may take you on by widening your horizons or lengthening your point of view or deepening your understanding or lifting your spirit' (p. 53). The use of storytelling in therapy is all about 'equipping people for the going'.

Barker (1996) rightly draws heavily on the work of Zeig (1980) in highlighting the key value of using metaphors, stories or anecdotes in psychotherapy. These are:

- making or illustrating points
- suggesting solutions to problems
- helping people to recognise themselves
- seeding ideas and increasing motivation
- controlling the therapeutic relationship
- embedding directives
- decreasing resistance
- reframing and redefining problems
- ego building
- modelling a way of communicating
- reminding people of their own resources
- desensitising people from their fears.

More generally, as Barker (1996) argues, metaphor and story can be deployed simply to establish rapport, establish treatment goals, programme for success through supportive metaphors or stories, mobilise indirection in making statements and hence reduce the likelihood of adverse results.

There has been a long history of the use of stories for educational purposes, not least in the parables of the New Testament of the Bible, where Christ encapsulated ways in which people should behave. In terms of longevity, many of the parables have lasted well. Even today, the story of the Good Samaritan continues to evoke powerfully the duty to help those in need. Such stories, Gunn and Fewell (1993) argue, 'can powerfully shape people's lives – even when the story may seem innocuous ... [they] have the potential to create new social worlds' (pp. 1–2). The didactic role of stories has perhaps been most evident in relation to the education of children. This takes place typically in the home, school or library where they are told fables and other stories that reveal and reinforce a truth or moral, or encourage preferred types of behaviour. In addition, the merits of stories spread much wider to their ability to teach other people about a wide variety of cultures, histories, geographies, lifestyles, personalities and so on. In fact, stories are one of the main carriers of knowledge within human society. Even outside the world of fiction, the structure of the story – with its beginning, middle and end – colonises the factual worlds of science and technology, and, indeed, writing factual books like this one!

Stories are a transformative force in people's lives, provoking self-reflection and change, and are profoundly human as Reissman (1993) indicates: 'Nature and the world do not tell stories; individuals do' (p. 2). But more than merely describe experience, stories build or construct it (Ricoeur, 1991). This constructive aspect of stories suggests they are an activity, in a similar way to how scholars, including Austin (1962), Searle (1969) and Grice (1975), identified aspects of speaking, such as promising, as 'speech acts'. We might think of 'story acts' – potentially changing our world or the world of others. Or we may think of this approach as 'applied stories'. It is a means by which we can 'redescribe reality' (Ricoeur, 1997) or, as Holmes (1995, p. 441) writes, it can lead to 'the assignment of positive meaning to what appear to be negative situations'. Indeed, we choose to view human life as an accomplishment of storytelling.

This book is intended as an introductory text for the wide range of people working in therapy, from psychotherapists and counsellors to various other professionals working in the field of mental health, and should also prove useful for all those with an interest in therapy or who wish to examine new ways of thinking about common mental health problems, such as depression or anxiety. The book capitalises on the growing interest in the healing power of stories or metaphors, which has attracted a diverse body of scholarship and interest (e.g. Bettelheim, 1976; Erickson et al., 1976; Rosen, 1982; Barker, 1985; Lankton & Lankton, 1989; Zeig & Gilligan, 1990; Parry & Doan, 1994; Pearce, 1996; Zimmerman & Dickerson, 1996; Dwivedi, 1997; Burns, 2001).

Our approach, then, fits within the cognitive behavioural model, commonly referred to as CBT, an area that has been written about extensively and is largely a self-help approach in which the client is helped to develop skills to manage specific problems to bring about desired changes in their lives. Thus the emphasis is on change rather than dwelling on the problem. A central principle of the approach is that the way in which a person acts is governed not only by the situation itself, but also by the individual's interpretation of such action. In psychological disturbance, the processing of this information is disordered and shows itself as distorted thinking or irrational beliefs. Individuals can learn to recognise this bias in thinking, leading to improvement in their symptoms.

There are certain assumptions that are fundamental to this approach. There is a focus on the client being educated in the model with all aspects of therapy being made explicit to the client. Therapy takes the form of a collaborative venture where client and therapist jointly plan strategies to overcome current problems within explicitly agreed goals. Integral to the therapy is that the problem solving in any particular area can then generalise to other situations. The therapist focuses on internal and external variables, which may not previously be seen as having relevance to the problem. These variables may include situational cues, affective states, behavioural cues, interpersonal factors, physiological factors and any maintaining factors. Implicit in this is that the major part of therapy takes place outside of the clinical setting as adaptive learning.

Beck (1979) and his colleagues, for example, developed a cognitive model of depression. In depression, there is a negative view of the self, the world and the future. Depressed individuals consider themselves to be inadequate and worthless, their surroundings seem bleak and uninteresting, and the future appears to be hopeless. This distortion of thinking causes further information to be similarly biased. Also, frequent negative automatic thoughts occur, which are spontaneous, plausible thoughts or images associated with unpleasant emotions. When viewed rationally these thoughts often turn out to be exaggerated and unrealistic. For instance, if a person was to forget an item of shopping, or spill a drink, they might respond by making a global self criticism, such as 'I'm stupid' or 'I can't do anything right'. Outside of this negative view of self, the individual might extend such thinking to negative views about the world or the future. In terms of the latter, with a future being perceived as bleak or hopeless, people can stop engaging in stimulating and rewarding activities and this can have a knock-on effect in terms of further depressing their mood. The cognitive model of depression suggests that assumptions developed in childhood become activated by a critical event and lead to cognitive disturbances. The careful application of alternative perspectives delivered by stories is another strategy to use within the CBT framework to deal with various maladaptive assumptions about the self, the world and the future.

Overall, cognitive behaviour therapy addresses what are referred to as the ABC's – the activating event or antecedents, beliefs and emotional consequences. Storytelling may have many varied applications within such therapy. For instance, even following education on the A-B-C principles many clients may maintain that certain factors in the situation (As) are responsible rather than any thought or belief. The As typically suggested as more powerful are physical environment, heredity and early childhood experiences. Further biochemistry or unconscious forces are frequently cited. The use of a story may help illustrate that these factors may predispose but not make the person behave in a particular way. Moreover, these factors may be overcome or lessened by the client's cognitions or beliefs. For instance, the therapist could tell the client about someone they know who has conquered a severe childhood experience. Importantly, in a wide range of CBT encounters, the unimposing nature of stories may circumvent resistance and opposition, particularly, for example, in the adolescent population. Because stories are less imposing, direct and authoritative, they are able to get under the radar as it were and influence change processes. Philip Barker (1996), citing the work of Sperry (1968) and Watzlawick (1978), argues that metaphor, the base metal of stories, whereby one thing represents another, can bypass the 'left brain' that acts as a logical 'watchdog', and, as with symbols and imagery, 'carry messages that can be applied to our present situation' (pp. 7–8). Metaphor, and its extension in longer narrative or story, assists human communication. For Barker, as for ourselves, metaphor and story offer a 'strategic' means of getting around various defences or blocks in securing therapeutic change.

In terms of story format, our main emphasis will be on the use of brief stories or anecdotes that introduce a limited number of characters, simple conventional plot (that is, ordering of events) and quick resolution or denouement (closure). We show how to utilise stories within a cognitive behavioural framework, while emphasising the storytelling power of the therapist. This differs, then, from the creative arts approaches to therapy in a tradition of story and metaphor (e.g. art and drama therapy, sand-tray work), which is largely client-centred and, as in Jungian approaches, where the 'story' would emanate from the client, not the therapist. It is also separate from, although linked to, the use of co-constructions of stories, where the therapist and client build stories together. In other words, while the therapist will determine which stories to introduce and when, this does not exclude the potential for the client to comment on the story and how it might apply to them, or how they would alter the story to have more relevance to them. In fact, we believe that therapist-led stories should not be delivered cold, as it were, but in a way that is open to refashioning or even replacement by other stories.

When we think of stories, we think of 'narrative', but there is a subtle difference. Narrative is the combination of story (form and substance of events, characters) and discourse (the form of expression and how it manifests itself in, for example, oral stories, film, drama) (see Chatman, 1978; Toolan, 1988). Toolan (1988) writes that a story or 'fabula' 'is a series of logically and chronologically related events that are caused or experienced by actors' (p. 9), while discourse is 'all the techniques that authors [or storytellers] bring to bear in their varying manner of presentation of the basic story' (p. 10). Thus narrative will include both story and discourse. Toolan continues: 'Story is the basic unshaped story material, and comprises events, characters, and settings. Story is a chronologically-ordered deep structure representation of all the primary and essential information concerning characters, events and settings, without which the narrative would not be well formed. The important point here is that this representation, or "bald version", is abstract but structured. We may then think of the teller of a narrative (the creative artist, the eye-witness, or whoever [the therapist]) as generating the "finished product", the presented discourse' (p. 13). Thus the storyteller may reorder any basic story into sequences that he or she feels will give the best performance.

A number of scholars have written about the structure of stories or narratives, not least Vladimir Propp (1968 [1928]), who famously identified 31 fundamental structures or elements of fairytales, and is one of many 'grammars' providing the rules for stories.

In his influential book, *The Morphology of the Folktale*, Propp interpreted about a hundred fairy tales in terms of what he called 'functions'. 'Function is understood as an act of character defined from the point of view of its significance for the course of the action' (Propp, 1928, p. 21). The 30 or so 'functions' he identified were the basic units of action. The folktales he analysed were, he claimed, all founded on the same simple formula (Chandler, 2001).

The basic tale typically begins with either injury to a victim, or the lack of some important object. Thus, at the very beginning, the end result is anticipated – it will consist in the retribution for the injury or the acquisition of what is missing. The hero, if he is not yet personally involved, is summoned. Once the hero is involved two further events generally take place.

First, he meets a 'donor'. This is often something or someone who is at first unappealing, such as a toad, a hag or a bearded old man, who tests the hero for the appropriate reaction, maybe for some courtesy or kindness or other motif to establish his moral qualities. The 'donor' then supplies the hero with a magical device, perhaps a ring, horse, cloak or lion, which enables him subsequently to pass victoriously through his ordeal.

Second, he meets the villain, monster or enemy, engaging him in the decisive combat. Yet, paradoxically enough, this episode, which would seem to be the central one, can be played out differently in some stories. An alternative track is sometimes taken in which the hero finds himself before a series of tasks or labours, which, with the help of his agent, he is ultimately able to solve properly.

The latter part of the tale often involves a series of retarding devices. For example, the hero may be pursued on his way home; another character, the 'false hero' may intrude and have to be thwarted, perhaps in the form of an unmasking of the false hero, with the ultimate transfiguration, marriage and perhaps even coronation of the hero himself. The hero then is transformed through action (Jameson, 1972, pp. 65–6; Chandler, 2001).

Roland Barthes (1977) noted that this emphasis on action and behaviour change in traditional folktales goes even deeper than this. Propp's approach has since been called 'structuralism', and structuralists tend to avoid defining human agents in terms of 'psychological essences'. Participants are defined by analysts not in terms of 'what they are' as 'characters' but in terms of 'what they do' (Barthes, 1977, p. 106). Propp listed seven *roles*: the *villain*; the *donor*; the *helper*; the *sought-for-person (and her father)*; the *dispatcher*; the *hero*; and the *false hero*.

Stories and narratives often have a conventional, established structure or genre. The sequence in which the storyteller presents events – the beginning, middle and end – is called the plot. As Scholes and Kellogg (1966) write: 'Plot is only the indispensable skeleton which, fleshed out with character and incident, provides the necessary clay into which life may be breathed' (p. 239). When listening to a storyteller, we have expectations of what we might hear. We view the story as a series of 'stepping stones' or 'plotting stones'. The story patterns of fairy tales, nursery tales, detective fiction, science fiction and romance, for example, should all be easily recognisable. With the fairy tale we would expect something along the lines of: 'Once upon a time there was a good princess who needed rescuing from a baddy. The good knight saves her and they ride off together and live happily ever after'. Or with a romance we expect: 'A boy meets a girl but the boy doesn't live up to expectations, she breaks away, he re-emerges later as an eligible mate, romance and marriage follow'. People in general are good at following plots, developing 'community-validated skills in specifying the more important characters and events in narratives. Most crucially of all, they get good at identifying what, relative to their own frameworks of world knowledge and cultural assumptions, is the "main point" of a story' (Scholes & Kellogg, 1966, p. 29). This competence means that the storyteller in therapy is not operating in expert isolation from the listener client. The listener client, as with most people, will be able to track and note a wide variety of universal storylines and plots. What is key is that the stories told are short, memorable and provide a transforming vision of desired thoughts and behaviours that a client may adopt for him or herself. Narration may be 'internal' or from the point of view within a character's consciousness; or 'external' where events and characters are described 'from a position outside of any of the protagonists' consciousnesses, with no privileged access to their private feelings and opinions' (Fowler, 1986; and see Toolan, 1988, p. 83). In any storytelling, it is vital to establish the setting, events and characters, although in short-story delivery, there is not the time to develop characters in any fulsome way. As Pratt (1977) argues (see Toolan, p. 175), there are 'differences of magnitude' between the narrative components of, say, novels and a 'brief oral narrative'. In therapy, the story needs to be literally 'telling', in other words, snappy and to the point. Furthermore, stories work best when applicable in a wider sense. As Toolan writes: 'the story's power rests in its generic truth, its pan-situational universality' (p. 103). This means stories with a core, universal message, rather like parables.

When telling stories, especially short stories or exemplars, we need to break the story into tidy chunks that are memorable. Narratives can be broken down into the following 'six pack' of components:

Abstract: What is the story about?
Orientation: Who is it about? When and where did it happen?
Complicating Action: What happened? Then what?
Evaluation: So what? Why is it important?
Result or Resolution: What happened in the end?
Coda: Why was this story worth telling?
(See Labov & Waletzky 1967; Labov, 1972; Labov 1982; Stubbs, 1983; Toolan, 1988)

The abstract outlines the story and is always abridged. As a socially situated activity, this phase of a story acts as a kind of request to carry on, rather like a trailer tempts you to view the whole film. Orientation sets the scene and gives sufficient information to intrigue the listener and raise interest. This is followed by Complicating Action, or a sequence of actions that enhance the tellability of the story. The Evaluation is where the point of the story is declared – its *raison d'être* – or what the storyteller is getting at. During the story, the storyteller will use various intensifiers, such as gestures, motions, expressive sounds, asides and repetitions to increase the impact of various elements. The storyteller may clarify details and amplify facts or descriptions. The storyteller may adopt the Conversational Historic Present, where events are presented as occurring at that moment. The Coda is the closure of the story – the 'that was that'. It may account in various ways for why the story was worth telling, for example, offering a moral or principle for how we might act in future. Polyani (1978) argued that the kinds of stories we tell reflect or disclose our cultural presuppositions and values. Indeed, the stories we tell will always carry political or ideological freight of one kind or another. As therapists, we need to monitor or police this aspect of storytelling to ensure that from an ethical point of view, we do not present material that is judgemental or prejudiced in any way to groups or individuals. The therapist needs to be especially sensitive to a variety of contexts in terms of the client's cultural background and mental state when telling stories. In other words, it is not just the stories we tell that are significant but the manner in which we do this. Care is required in tailoring language to the audience and adjusting to any differences in background knowledge. The more knowledge, values, attitudes and beliefs that our audience shares with us as storytellers, the more they will understand and the less chance there is of having a negative impact.

Tannen (1979) identifies 'structures of expectation' based on past experiences, which influence the way we construct stories or interpret them, while Denzin (1989) argues that people's narratives often become transformed into 'epiphanies' or manifestations that alter the meaning of a person's life. As such they can be a kind of threshold between one way of telling about the self and another. The 'truth' or 'meaning' behind any life may be continuously refashioned and reshaped or revised through story. This process is a kind of 'sense-making', with individuals defining themselves in a particular way through their narratives.

In terms of psychotherapy, the term narrative is frequently presented in the composite 'narrative therapy', where client's stories are explored and reframed in new and positive ways. Fundamental to this field is the examination of how people make sense of the world through storytelling or, indeed, how their actions are scripted like a narrative, and how clients may benefit from help in co-constructing and re-authoring their narratives (Sarbin, 1990; Bruner, 1990; McNamee & Gergen, 1992; Reissman, 1993; Parry & Doan, 1994; Rennie, 1994; Saleebey, 1994; Wigren, 1994; Zimmerman & Dickerson, 1996; Smith & Nylund, 1997). Parry and Doan (1994), for example, promote therapy that involves the client 'deconstructing' their life story and revising or 're-visioning' it. As Brown et al. (1996) indicate: 'This "strong form" of the narrative turn in therapeutic discourse works alongside similar developments on a variety of fronts. There are narrative approaches developing in a number of areas' (p. 1570), such as survivors of domestic violence or incest, and eating disorders. As we maintain elsewhere: 'Including some acknowledgement of the storied, subjective, linguistic nature of distress and treatment, then, is increasingly modish' (Brown et al., 1996, p. 1571).

Our approach, however, is from a different direction to this therapeutic tradition. It is concerned with the therapist as storyteller rather than the client. Our divergence with 'narrative therapy' stems, then, from the agency of storytelling and partly from the belief, as we have noted elsewhere, that those whose work 'is informed by the use of narrative metaphors often have well-developed accounts of what the clients' stories mean, how they get produced, the dynamics of the therapeutic relationship, power in therapy, and the interpretations they can draw' (Crawford et al., 1998, p. 114). In other words, just as creative writing courses can help students of literature understand literature from the inside, so too the development and use of stories by therapists for therapeutic purposes can extend an understanding of client's stories.

Makari and Shapiro (1994) advocate attending to the client's unspoken, unconscious or 'shadow narrative'. Rennie (1994) is similarly traditional and confident in referring to the self-aware, storytelling subjectivity of clients. Such confidence is extended by those, like Gross (1995), who consider clients as having power over therapists: 'Patients present with a set of pragmatic needs and wants and they teach therapists how to help them' (Gross, 1995, p. 182). Therapist-led storytelling does not necessarily oppose such dynamics. In fact, it may open a pathway to empowerment, while increasing rapport and normalisation at the same time. After all, storytelling as an activity may demystify or soften the professional–client boundary in a way that advances therapeutic benefits, not least by the powerful effects of indirection. While Rennie (1994, p. 241) ironically exhorts therapists to be 'patient' when clients are telling a story, this should not detract from the positive effects of the therapists delivering the story themselves.

That said, whatever the agency of storytelling, both therapists and clients in this context are never as fully empowered and autonomous as we might suppose. The stories clients tell and therapists tell clients will always reflect the interests of the teller and reflect the context in which they were created, not least professional and cultural processes. In terms of the latter, clients come to therapy having already absorbed a great deal of the therapeutic ways of assigning meaning and narrating their various problems or difficulties. The therapist herself takes an evaluative stance and manages client narratives to focus on 'deep', 'underlying' or 'masked' issues. In practice, despite the voice of user-empowerment, clients in therapy are not merely left to their own devices. As Bruner (1984) writes: 'A life as told, a life history, is a narrative, influenced by the cultural conventions of telling, by the audience, and by the social context' (p. 7). Thus, therapists will need to be aware that a wide variety of contexts will influence the making and reception of stories, not least their interpretation.

Our approach seeks to encourage therapists to utilise the educational and transformational power of stories in guiding their clients to beneficial changes in attitudes, emotions, behaviour and self conception or image. However, we do not wish to imply that these are discrete or stand-alone categories and acknowledge the overlap and influence between these areas.

In addition to providing a model to guide the change process, stories also promote self reflection, communication, working together and memory. They are invaluable resources in the therapist's 'tool box' regardless of theoretical background, novice or expert status. In formal and informal 'therapy', stories can be applied to everyday difficulties, and to particular mental health problems such as anxiety, depression, obsessive compulsive disorder and so on.

Therapists, and people in general, will often employ anecdotes in therapeutic or transformative ways, yet may be unaware of just how powerful this can be. They may be limited in this valuable activity by the range of anecdotes available to them from their own resources and creativity, or those derived from various books. This book provides a much-needed theoretical and practical resource about therapist-led brief stories and metaphors – a fitting room (although by no means comprehensive) for the therapist to try on stories and anecdotes – that may be suitable for doing work with people with particular mental health problems. The brevity or conciseness of stories both aids memory of key concepts rather than belabouring explicit detail of what happened in terms of characters and plot. They are also time sensitive, something that is significant when client waiting lists for many therapists are difficult to manage. In addition, the application of brief stories and metaphors is a useful method to teach complex skills and models of therapeutic approaches and enhance therapy itself.

We will define and explain how brief anecdotes or stories can be used – providing summaries of the way they can be applied and the kinds of problems they can be used to address. In addition there are techniques that storytellers use in the theatre or the classroom, which can usefully be appropriated by therapists, for example: by using changes in vocal tone, tempo and rate of utterance; incorporating affective involvement; and matching the client's personal affect with those of the characters. In addition, the reader will learn about the need for using or developing compelling story lines that are enjoyable, tailored for the client, delivered with enthusiasm, and which provoke both parties to think in new and challenging ways. Finally, the reader will be alerted to the need to rehearse stories, practise their delivery, observe client responses and ensure that such an approach does not become evasive, condescending or irrelevant.

In order to examine the kinds of traditions in psychotherapy and the treatment styles where some kind of story or other has been deployed, let us begin with the field of cognitive behavioural therapy and discuss the elements of this approach that are effective and the contribution that stories might make to this, and then describe some other therapeutic styles, which involve either the therapist telling the client a story or the clients reading stories for themselves.

USING METAPHORS AND STORIES IN COGNITIVE BEHAVIOUR THERAPY

Cognitive restructuring

The use of stories in cognitive behaviour therapy may take the form of cognitive restructuring, inasmuch as it involves giving clients some sort of framework to make sense of their situation and offering them alternative and less distressing formulations of what is happening to them. An important strand in our argument is that this process of cognitive restructuring is central to cognitive behaviour therapy – indeed it is described as one of the 'core interventions' in the cognitive behavioural repertoire (Bor et al., 2001).

The effectiveness of cognitive restructuring, either on its own or in combination with other techniques, has been demonstrated across a range of psychological difficulties and therapeutic styles. To select a few examples from a very large literature, cognitive restructuring forms part of an effective intervention programme for depression (e.g. Sanderson & McGinn, 2001; Miller et al., 2002), conditions involving anxiety, panic and fear (Marks, 2002) and post traumatic stress disorders (Grey et al., 2002). As well as the well-known territory of classic depressive and anxiety conditions, cognitive restructuring is finding a role in a variety of more specific problems such as fear of flying (Bor et al., 2001), recovery from child abuse (Smucker et al., 2002) and social phobia (Franklin et al., 2001) to name but a few of the wide range of problems this therapeutic model is used for. In terms of specific hints in the clinical and research literature about the use of stories and literature, a paper by Moller and

Steel (2002) reports a study of cognitive restructuring in adult survivors of child sex abuse, where the use of bibliotherapy (which we discuss further below) is mentioned as part of the cognitive restructuring strategy. The task of resolving sadness among young women, as studied by Gramling and McCain (1997), involves the substitution of life stories, which fully engage with the complexities of adulthood and resolve the loss of former dreams and ambitions.

Thus, with cognitive restructuring being an effective part of the cognitive behavioural approach, stories can be used to enhance or consolidate this aspect of the therapeutic process to the benefit of both clients and therapists.

Memorability, homework and compliance

The memorability of stories and anecdotes also has a bearing on the effectiveness of therapy between the formal sessions with the therapist. The use of homework between sessions is a widely used adjunct in many therapeutic regimes and anything that increases the ease and likely compliance with homework will very likely improve the effectiveness of therapy.

There is good evidence that the use of homework assignments – and, more importantly, clients' compliance with them – in cognitive behavioural therapy regimes, increases the effectiveness of therapy (Karantzis & Lampropoulos, 2002). Moreover, the development of therapeutic skill in making homework assignments attractive to the client has been encouraged by a number of authors (e.g. Tomkins, 2002). Thus, anything that helps the ease of use or memorability of the new strategies, which the therapist is trying to encourage, will be of benefit to both clients and therapists. If, for example, one is trying to encourage the blocking of negative thoughts, the attitude of collaborative empiricism to challenge negative cognitions or even grander projects such as the reconstruction of self image, the practice of new habits of thought is crucial. The availability of a coherent story that reminds clients of the practice and directs them towards the therapeutic goals can be used to make the homework readily remembered and easy to execute.

Moreover, in connection with this, one of the problems of examining and challenging underlying dysfunctional beliefs is that they are less likely to be reported when the client's mood is positive (Persons & Miranda, 2002). As Persons and Miranda argue, the concern is that any apparent change in the belief system is an artefact of the change in mood, and the basic dysfunctional beliefs may remain unchallenged by the therapy. The virtue of stories and anecdotes as an aid to therapy is that they may be called to mind relatively independently of the client's mood and may be effective in challenging negative thoughts, whatever the client's mood at the time. Appropriately selected stories in therapy may thus be used to consolidate progress towards therapeutic goals because of their memorability and their ability to outperform the negative automatic thoughts, which are believed to be important in depression and anxiety disorders.

The memorability of stories, then, can work in their favour. If a story or an apt metaphor is readily called to mind, then this makes the technique the story embodies more available to the client, especially in situations where the rehearsal of new and more adaptive strategies is important.

STORIES AND BIBLIOTHERAPY

Stories have been used most explicitly and extensively within the school of psychotherapy known as bibliotherapy. This is defined by Cohen (1994, p. 40) as 'the therapeutic use of literature with guidance or intervention from a therapist'. Adding to this, Bhattacharya (1997, p. 14) suggests that literature is used 'with a therapeutic outcome in mind. Literature related to illness or problems, as well as fiction or poetry, may be incorporated as a therapeutic adjunct in order to help patients gain knowledge and insight ...'. It is possible to look to this tradition as a way of offering some sort of evaluation of the value of briefer anecdotes, such as we are advocating in this volume. Bruno Bettelheim (e.g. 1976) was one of the key authors advocating this approach, principally with fairy stories in therapy for children. Subsequently, a number of authors such as Sarbin (1986), Bruner (1990) and therapists such as White and Epston (1990) have advocated the use of narratives from the humanities, especially literature and the theatre.

There is thus a growing interest in the role that stories of a more extended literary kind can play in therapy. Whereas we are promoting the use of relatively brief anecdotes, and the genre of therapeutic writing we are discussing under this heading is concerned with longer pieces of fiction, the parallels are nevertheless persuasive. As one recent promoter of this kind of resource, Knights (1995) has argued 'reading is one way of gaining experience of the making of meanings in all their overlapping contexts, deepening attention to the potentials of humanness can be explored and developed' (p. 3). What he says about books can just as well be said about stories: 'the knowledge we engage with in books is at least in some respects similar to the knowledge we need to possess about people' (ibid., p. 3).

The use of stories in the form of novels and plays has been promoted in family therapies too. For example, Androutsopoulou (2001) argues persuasively that stories originating elsewhere in the culture can be used as 'safe vehicles' for people to talk about their own lives, experiences and emotions. Further, people in therapy might themselves bring in stories derived from books, films, plays and television programmes, which, as McLeod (1997) puts it, might help them 'bring more sense and meaning to their own personal narrative' (p. 126). Indeed, if the client mentions any stories in this way, the therapist can make valuable deductions here about the kind of story that appeals to the client.

In addition, there is an argument that the use of stories might facilitate the client in expressing aspects that might be bad, taboo or transgressive (Coulacoglou, 1988). Crompton (1992) argues that people, even younger clients, do not identify with characters in stories, but 'recognise through [their] response to [characters'] behaviour and the feelings [they] attribute to them, their own so far unexpressed feelings' (p. 138) and perhaps learn some possible 'ways of managing' (p. 139) the emotional and moral difficulty. Indeed, fiction is believed to help people develop a way of talking about experiences that have been silenced or marginalised (Parry, 1991). There is a strong consensus of opinion that literature, in the form of folktales especially, can help clients express feelings and conflicts 'safely' (Dwivedi, 1997; Gersie, 1997; McArdle & Byrt, 2001).

Androutsopoulou (2001) notes that clients appear especially to like stories that represent breakthroughs, that is, stories where clients can see the story characters 'have resisted, have finally broken loose from dominant narrative (life) patterns imposed on them by their families, their community or society in general. As a result, characters feel free to do or become whatever they most wish' (p. 286).

POETRY THERAPY

Poetry therapy is a therapeutic mode whose effectiveness is well established. Some of this involves clients writing their own poems, but equally, a good deal of it involves exposing people to the poems of others. A poem, in some respects, is like an anecdote in that it condenses a brief narrative, perhaps about events, problems or feelings and draws, like a story, on images, literary motifs and generic conventions. Indeed, as prose may be poetic, and sometimes poems resemble stories, it is difficult to draw a sharp distinction between the two literary forms. Thus, what is said about the effectiveness of using poetry in therapy may equally well be said about stories and anecdotes.

In terms of how poetry is used, as Hedberg (1997, p. 93) explains: 'In a clinical setting, the poetry therapist leads the group in teaching patients to experience poetry, and other bibliotherapeutic materials as a means of self expression and ventilation of feelings.'

This form of therapy, whose effectiveness is relatively well established, may be efficacious in achieving a good many ends that psychotherapists and their clients might find desirable. It is effective in '... maintaining patient wellbeing, preventing decompensation and sustaining recovery' (Hedberg, 1997, p. 93). More specifically, therapy using poetry is believed to lead to four kinds of benefit, namely affective, cognitive, personal and interpersonal development (Lerner, 1975; 1981; 1994; 1996; Mazza et al., 1987; Hynes & Hynes-Berry, 1994). According to Hedberg (1997), poetry – and, we would argue, stories – can aid with such psychotherapeutic tasks as catharsis, modelling, reframing, enriching and amplifying feeling content, opening up the possibility of hope. Poetry – and stories – have the ability to communicate learning, humour, insight and improve the verbalisation of feelings (Mazza, 1993; 2003; Lerner, 1994; 1996; Fox, 1995; Rossiter, 1996; Chavis, 2003). Moreover, argues Hedberg (1997), it is possible to improve interpersonal skills through greater non-judgemental acceptance and understanding of self and others.

HYPNOTHERAPY AND HYPNOTIC INDUCTIONS

Hypnosis is a difficult and controversial subject to introduce, not least because it is not entirely clear what it is. In very general terms, it is defined by Pratt et al. (1988) as a state of highly focused attention or trance in which external stimuli are disattended and suggestions become more effective than usual. Hypnotherapy has been used for many of the same kinds of issues and problems as cognitive behaviour therapy. On the face of it at least, it shares many of the same practical features. In a similar way, both may employ relaxation techniques, explore a client's feelings about the presenting problem and seek to substitute a less distressing coping strategy. Hypnotherapy has been used successfully in dealing with self destructive habits of thought, ameliorating anxiety disorders and treating pain (Zarren & Eimer, 2002). Social phobias have been dealt with successfully (Schoenberger et al., 1997), postoperative pain has been reduced and recovery enhanced (Mauer et al., 1999), and sexual adjustment has been improved in couples therapy (Araoz et al., 2001). Indeed, any brief survey can only scratch the surface of these versatile techniques.

The reason why we are including it here is that not only is it a therapy with some demonstrable effectiveness, it uses what practitioners call 'hypnotic inductions', but which we might better call stories or anecdotes. From the stage hypnotist's traditional 'You are feeling very sleepy', to the variety of stories, myths and inductive strategies used in clinical practice today, the technique involves gaining and holding the client's attention and inducing them to participate in the story. Most interestingly, there are favourable reports in the literature of practitioners using techniques very similar to those we are advocating. For example, Kroger and Fezler (2002) describe using guided imagery – and what is a story if not a therapeutically guided set of images? – as a relaxation technique in their synthesis of hypnotic and behavioural therapies. Successful reports of this kind of guided imagery technique also come from clinicians who have used it to treat post traumatic stress disorder (Jiranek, 2000). The use of stories to shift cognitions has been described in the hypnotherapy literature by Mendelovic and Doron (2001), who called their strategy the story within a story technique. Here they create a primary story in which a secondary story is embedded. The embedded secondary story is deliberately confusing, perhaps as the characters do things which appear stupid or spiteful, whereas the primary story appears reality based and contains the 'better' way of thinking about the situation.

These uses of stories, then, although they come from a different therapeutic tradition than the one in which we are based, are suggestive of the usefulness of certain kinds of storytelling in therapy. Indeed, to call a storytelling event a 'hypnotic induction' may well surround it in mystery or make it appear offputting. Stories, at least, have the virtue of being unthreatening. Also, this brief consideration of the current work ongoing in hypnotherapy can perhaps serve to reassure the reader concerned about evidence of effectiveness. Where we wish to tread, others have gone before, in many cases with some success.

THEORETICAL CONSIDERATIONS IN STORYTELLING: TELLING THE STORY OF WHY IT WORKS

There is a long-standing respect for the therapeutic use of stories within psychotherapy. The origins of storytelling are ancient (Wenckus, 1994; Hinds,

1997) and many of the originators of psychotherapy themselves have made extensive use of stories as a way of making sense of clients' predicaments, especially Freud (1908/1985), who put the benefits of reading literature in the following terms: 'our actual enjoyment of an imaginative work proceeds from a liberation of tensions … enabling us … to enjoy our daydreams without self reproach or shame' (p. 141).

The contemporary rationale for including stories in therapy is perhaps most fully elaborated by theorists who adopt a narrative approach. Kenneth Gergen (1994, p. 185) explains the importance and inevitability of 'borrowing' narrative forms:

'Most of us begin our encounters with stories in childhood. Through fairy tales, folktales, and family stories we receive our first organised accounts of human action. Stories continue to absorb us as we read novels, biography and history, they occupy us at the movies, at the theatre and on television. And possibly because of this intimate and longstanding acquaintanceship, stories also serve as a critical means by which we make ourselves intelligible within the social world.' Thus, although Gergen does not evaluate the effectiveness of the use of stories, he nevertheless makes a persuasive argument about their utility.

Kenneth Gergen's partner Mary has shared this interest in stories and their role in human conduct. She focuses specifically on the form of stories as a way of making sense of their role as transformative agents. She suggests that 'traditions of storytelling, dramatic performance, literature and the like have generated a range of culturally shared forms of emplotment.' These stories, most importantly, may take the form of (i) stability, where life is monotonous and directionless, (ii) progression, where life is getting better and (iii) regression, where life is getting worse. These narratives, as well as being visible in the cultural artefacts of Western civilization, may entrap individuals. Gergen (1994) notes that people who are in the grip of a stability self narrative might benefit from psychotherapy and Androutsopoulou (2001) notes that people might become trapped in a regression self narrative and might also benefit from the transformative effects of therapy. Whereas we are not focusing on the varieties of psychotherapy that emphasise the clients' narratives, we are nevertheless drawing on some of the same theoretical foundations in order to develop a rationale for what we are recommending. From this perspective, then, people may find themselves in the grip of stories that are unhappy, destructive or dysfunctional. It is only a small leap of logic to move from this to the suggestion that maybe better stories might lead to the betterment of the human condition, at least for some clients.

In fields outside psychotherapy, too, the use of small, self contained anecdotes in one form or another is gaining ground rapidly. A paper by Leber and Vanoli (2001) details for example the use of jokes and funny stories in occupational therapy. The use of humorous anecdotes, according to their informants, was thought of positively. Even more interestingly, the use of humorous stories was thought of more positively by the more experienced therapists in Leber and Vanoli's study. Again, jokes and humorous anecdotes are not exactly the same as what we are trying to promote here, but it is noteworthy that the greater the experience of the practitioner the greater the respect for these techniques.

There are, as we have tried to indicate, many examples in the form of case reports and studies where clients have apparently benefited from the use of literature or poetry. Whereas this is not exactly coextensive with the kinds of anecdotes we are promoting in this volume, some of the therapeutic functions might be similar. For example, Jones (1997) describes the use of poetry in helping a woman with terminal cancer, where he concludes that the poetry gave the client '. . . a meaningful language through which it became possible to conceive what, under ordinary circumstances, could not be conceived, and committing such understanding to words' (Jones, 1997, p. 243).

The use of stories in therapy has proved difficult to evaluate in formal terms. A number of authors have noted that evaluative research in therapies using literature has been limited, partly because of the sheer number of variables involved (Harrower, 1978; McArdle & Byrt, 2001). The conclusions reached by Jensen and Blair (1997, p. 525) are still true today, some six years later: 'Most published works cannot be compared and contrasted, due to the vastly differing: (a) definitions of therapy; (b) uses of reading, writing, performing and listening; and (c) assumptions on which the research/opinion was based. . . . The terminology surrounding the research area is marked by contradiction and confusion. Terms . . . were, at times, used interchangeably, yet were also used specifically in regard to groups, actions, and processes that were decidedly different.'

Despite this confusion and inconsistency there are a number of studies, which have reported positive outcomes as a result of bibliotherapy and poetry therapy (see McArdle & Byrt, 2001). The conclusion is, predictably, that more research is needed. Moreover, no method appears to be effective with all clients (Mazza, 1993; McGibon, 1996). Determining clinical effectiveness, according to Cohen (1994), will involve determining which clients derive most benefit and which interventions are most effective given the goals of a particular programme of therapy. However, looking further afield, to the related spheres of cognitive behavioural therapy, poetry therapy, bibliotherapy and hypnotherapy can give us some clues as to the aspects of storytelling in therapy that will be effective.

EVIDENCE-BASED PRACTICE WHEN USING STORIES IN THERAPY

The spirit in which psychotherapy is given and received in the UK and US has recently undergone a revolution, in that practitioners, managers, policymakers and clients themselves are increasingly likely to demand evidence of its effectiveness. Moreover, for any innovation in therapy to gain acceptance in this climate, it is necessary for practitioners and policymakers to be convinced of its effectiveness on the client group in question. The spirit of evidence-based practice pervades much current thinking on health in the UK and US, and forms a centrepiece of the British government's strategy for the health service (Department of Health, 1996) and the National Service Framework for Mental Health (Department of Health, 1999).

In the light of this, let us turn our attention to the evidence for the effectiveness of stories in therapy. Because this kind of approach has been developed only relatively recently we do not have a substantial evidence base. Our purpose in this book is to introduce the approach rather than to present the results of a finished research programme. Evidence-based practice tends to favour approaches that have accumulated a long line of 'evidence' after all, at the expense of more tentative and innovative approaches.

However, we can secure reasonable foundations of the approach we are recommending in this volume. The use of stories, if successful, can contribute to aspects of therapy that have already been demonstrated to be effective in relieving clients' distress and making them more self-reliant, more resourceful in tackling life's difficulties and resolving traumatic experiences. However, direct assessments of the effectiveness of stories in therapy have not, as far as we know, been performed. Certainly, it has been difficult to locate evidence from randomised controlled trials of such a therapeutic strategy.

Let us begin by trying to define evidence-based practice, and then give some indication of the evidence there is against which we can judge the likely effectiveness of incorporating stories and anecdotes into therapy.

The tenets of evidence-based practice are notoriously difficult to apply systematically to psychotherapy (Reynolds, 2000). Defining what evidence-based practice involves has itself proved controversial. One of the widely quoted definitions is provided by Sackett et al. (1997), who define evidence-based practice in medicine as '… the conscientious, explicit and judicious use of current best evidence in making decisions about the care of individual patients based on skills which allow the doctor to evaluate both personal experience and external evidence in a systematic and objective manner' (p. 71).

This definition is seen as one of the more liberal ones because it includes the clinician's personal experience as well as the 'external evidence'. The key feature of applying evidence-based models, according to Reynolds (2000, p. 258), is not necessarily the exclusive reliance on external evidence, but more the clinician being 'careful and thoughtful, … able to justify their decisions to other people (colleagues, the patients or their family) and should use their judgement in reaching a decision on the basis of their own experience and the evidence.' Although the emphasis on clinical judgement here invites a kind of evidence that is supported by our clinical experience, the question of evidence-based practice is still a difficult one for any new style of therapy to crack. The major reason for this difficulty is the hierarchy of evidence that many policymakers, researchers and clinicians rely upon. That is, as Guyatt et al. (1995) put it, the pyramid of evidence looks like this, with the most credible kind at the top:

1. Systematic reviews and meta analysis.
2. Randomised controlled trials with definitive results.
3. Randomised controlled trials with non-definitive results.
4. Cohort studies.
5. Case control studies.

6. Cross sectional studies.
7. Case reports.

Whereas we cannot find evidence that satisfies the higher orders of the scheme promoted by Guyatt et al. (1995), there are a number of reports of effective therapies that do employ comparable techniques. Some of these certainly involve comparisons of treatment and control groups, and can lead us to an educated opinion that using stories in therapy might be effective. One of the problems in evaluating the effectiveness of the use of stories in therapy is that while these techniques have been widely employed, they have often grown up in a haphazard fashion and have not been formally evaluated. We do know, however, that using stories to convey psychological concepts has been around since psycho therapy began, and as McMullin (2000, p. 423) notes there has been some research into the effectiveness of the use of stories in therapy (Lazarus, 1971; 1989; 1995; Singer, 1974; 1976; 1995; Singer & Pope, 1978; Sheikh & Shaffer, 1979; Sheikh, 1983a; 1983b), the value of analogies and metaphors in therapy (Siegelman, 1990; Martin et al., 1992; McCurry & Hayes, 1992; Donnelly & Dumas, 1997), and a number of scholars examine the therapeutic use of fantasy (Leuner, 1969; Shorr, 1972; 1974; Gordon, 1978; Duhl, 1983).

APPLYING STORIES IN PRACTICE

Can anyone be a good storyteller? What is required to tell stories well? Perhaps the key requirements are good communication skills that include imagination, enthusiasm and being sensitive to the needs of the listener. But what are we looking for in any story we choose and how do we perform it?

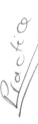

Wright (1995, pp. 14–21) has identified key elements to the art of storytelling that can be adapted as follows for therapeutic work:

Telling stories

- Give the client something personal, not just something out of a book.
- Respond to the client and watch for lack of comprehension.
- Use your body and gestures to heighten meaning.
- Use language that the client knows.
- Use good variety with your voice in terms of pitch, volume, intonation, rhythm, softness/harshness, pace and pause.

Choosing stories

- Use stories that quickly engage the client.
- Find stories that you like and can tell well.
- Identify appropriate stories.
- Make sure the story is understandable.
- Tune in to the client and fit the story to the therapeutic occasion.

Remembering a story

- Learn by heart the key elements of the story, not every detail.
- Read the story several times and practise retelling it to a friend or tape-recorder.
- Select and note down key points as a 'story skeleton'.
- Keep a file of these 'story skeletons' and use them as a memory aid to support recall.
- File each card according to their therapeutic purpose.
- Obtain measurements from the client of the story's usefulness and add this information to 'story skeletons'.

In terms of techniques for using the full potential of your voice, language and body when storytelling, Wright makes several useful recommendations:

- Sit so you can breathe easily – not 'hunched up'.
- Keep breathing while talking to avoid breathlessness.
- Adopt different voices as required, depending on the range of characters.
- At key moments use pause to increase tension, mark key points, activate the listener to fill in the gaps, predict what you might say next and digest what has been said.
- Ensure you are confident how to begin and end the story.
- Omit, add, change and emphasise elements of the story if you have a good reason.
- Reinforce actions within the story with movements, gestures and mimicry.
- Involve the client in the story (if appropriate) – perhaps by pretending to give them something etc.
- Make your movements slow and simple.
- Look at the client rather than merely scan his or her face.

Teresa Grainger (1997) presents further useful tips, adapted below:

- Keep in your mind images from the story as 'landmarks' or 'comic strips' in sequential order.
- Recall sensory aspects of the scenes (smell, sound, sight, taste and touch) to help spoken evocation and description.
- Photocopy chosen story and divide into chunks, highlighting key phrases and adding notes in the margins.
- Ensure key phrases from the story are recalled accurately to keep their impact.

Being good at telling stories is one thing, but having a good story to tell is another. It is vital that the therapist begins to identify stories for certain purposes or functions, whether it is to change people's attitudes, emotions, behaviour, self image and so on. At the same time, she will need to pay attention to what makes a good story in and of itself, that is, such things as plot (however simple), characters, setting and atmosphere. Whichever story a therapist chooses to narrate to influence a client's thinking, it must be compelling, interesting and hence memorable. By being memorable, it is far more likely that the client will have a 'takeaway' version that can influence them long after the particular therapeutic session.

In her early influential book, *The Way of the Storyteller*, Ruth Sawyer (1942) wrote: 'Unquestionably a large measure of the success of the storyteller depends on his selection of stories, his power to discriminate, his growing ability to evaluate' (p. 151). This applies equally to storytelling in therapy. The therapist can begin to establish herself as a storyteller by background reading of tales and stories that might be adaptable for therapeutic purposes. By collecting these stories, she can begin to explore how best to use them, adding new ones as she progresses, or discarding those which are less effective in communicating new ways for clients to think and behave.

As Rosenwald and Ochberg (1992) argue: 'Personal stories are not merely a way of telling someone (or oneself) about one's life, they are the means by which identities may be fashioned' (p. 1). In this sense, we might argue for the potential for stories delivered by therapists to refashion the identities of clients – to reorder, redesign or reshape internalised stories about their identity – change their histories, alter unhelpful or negative emphasis, speak what has been omitted, question their identities as protagonists or victims.

Ultimately, as McMullin (2000) writes, any story 'must contain within it at least the essence of a bridge between the client's old, damaging belief and a new, preferred belief' (p. 418). Adapting Barker (1996) and Burns (2001) we may create a checklist of things to consider when using stories in therapy:

- establish rapport with the client before storytelling
- acknowledge the role of storytelling within any overarching therapeutic approach, e.g. psychoanalysis, cognitive behaviour therapy etc.
- acquire full and detailed knowledge of the client and agree therapeutic goals before using storytelling as a major intervention in therapy
- determine whether indirect storytelling is the best strategy to resolve a client's problem rather than the use of more direct interventions
- identify the clinical use of an anecdote or story that would best apply to the client based on previous cases and evidence base
- view storytelling as only a part of an intervention plan
- introduce storytelling as a normal part of therapy and prepare clients for this milieu
- avoid story content that may have negative connotations for the client
- avoid using stories as a 'standard package' for every client and every problem
- tailor the story to different clinical situations (including time limitations), client's personality and mental state, cultural background, preferred sensory channels, language or communication styles, and topic and story preferences revealed in metaphors and stories delivered by clients themselves
- observe feedback and keep notes for future reference
- learn from any mistakes you make in using stories.

In *Storytelling in Therapy* we are not introducing something entirely new in terms of therapy – therapists have long been using stories to good effect – however, this book attempts to bring into the foreground the use of therapeutic stories in a variety of situations/problem areas. For some therapists telling stories may be rather challenging or problematic, perhaps because they have not taken this approach before or are concerned that their stories may be inappropriate or patronising. This book provides examples of stories for use by both inexperienced and more skilled storytellers, and indicates how these can be deployed for specific therapeutic purposes.

REFERENCES

Androutsopoulou, A. (2001) Fiction as an aid to therapy: A narrative and family rationale for practice. *Journal of Family Therapy*, **23**, 278–95.

Araoz, D., Burte, J. & Goldin, E. (2001) Sexual hypnotherapy for couples and family counsellors. *Family Journal of Counselling and Therapy for Couples and Families*, 9(1), 75–81.

Austin, J. L. (1962) *How to do things with words*. Oxford: Clarendon Press.

Barker, P. (1985) *Using metaphors in psychotherapy*. New York: Brunner/Mazel.

Barker, P. (1996) *Psychotherapeutic metaphors: A guide to theory and practice*. New York: Brunner/Mazel.

Barthes, R. (1977) *Image, music, text*. London: Fontana.

Beck, A. J. (1979) *Cognitive therapy and the emotional disorder*. New York: Meridian Books.

Bettelheim, B. (1976) *The uses of enchantment: The meaning and importance of fairy tales*. New York: Knopf.

Bhattacharyya, A. (1997) Historical backdrop. In K. N. Dwivedi (Ed.) *The therapeutic use of stories*. London: Routledge.

Bor, R., Parker, J. & Papadopoulos, L. (2001) Brief, solution focused treatment sessions for clients with a fear of flying. *Counselling Psychology Review*, 16(4), 32–40.

Brown, B., Nolan, P., Crawford, P. & Lewis, A. (1996) Interaction, language and the 'Narrative Turn' in psychotherapy and psychiatry. *Social Science and Medicine*, 43(11), 1569–78.

Bruner, E. M. (1984) The opening up of anthropology. In E. M. Bruner (Ed.). *Text, play and story: The construction and reconstruction of self and society*. Washington: American Ethnological Society.

Bruner, J. (1990) *Acts of meaning*. Cambridge, Mass.: Harvard University Press.

Burns, G. W. (2001) *101 healing stories: Using metaphors in therapy*. New York: Wiley & Sons.

Chandler, D. (2001) *Semiotics: the basics*. London: Routledge.

Chatman, S. (1978) *Story and discourse: Narrative structure in fiction and film*. Ithaca and London: Cornell University Press.

Chavis, G. G. (2003) *The healing fountain: poetry therapy for life's journey*. Saint Cloud, MN: North Star Press of Saint Cloud.

Cohen, L. J. (1994) Bibliotherapy: a valid treatment modality. *Journal of Psychosocial Nursing and Mental Health Services*, 32(9), 40–4.

Coulacoglou, C. (1988) Identification and socialization in fairy tales. *Routes to Literature for Children and Young Adults*, 9, 13–16.

Crawford, P., Brown, B. & Nolan, P. (1998) *Communicating care: The language of nursing*. Cheltenham: Nelson Thornes.

Crompton, J. (1992) *Children and counselling*. London: Arnold.

Denzin, N. K. (1989) *Interpretive biography*, Qualitative Methods Series, 17. London: Sage.

Department of Health (1996) Towards an evidence based service. London: Department of Health.

Department of Health (1999) A national service framework for mental health. London: Department of Health.

Donnelly, C. & Dumas, J. (1997) Use of analogies in therapeutic situations: An analog study. *Psychotherapy*, **34**(2), Summer, 124–32.

Duhl, B. (1983) *From the inside out and other metaphors*. New York: Brunner/Mazel.

Dwivedi, K. N. (Ed.)(1997) *The therapeutic use of stories*. London: Routledge.

Erickson, M. H., Rossi, E. L. & Rossi, S. (1976) *Hypnotic realities*. New York: Irvington.

Fowler, R. (1986) *Linguistic criticism*. Oxford: Oxford University Press.

Fox, J. (1995) *Finding what you didn't lose*. New York: Tarcher/Putnam.

Franklin, M. E., Feeny, N. C., Abramowitz, J. S., Zoellner, L. A. & Bux, D. A. (2001) Comprehensive cognitive behaviour therapy: A multicomponent treatment for generalized social phobia. *Psicoterapia cognitive e comportamentale*, 7(3), 211–21.

Freud, S. (1908/1985) Creative writers and daydreaming. In A. Dickson (Ed.). *Art and literature 'Jensen's gradiva', 'Leonardo Da Vinci' and other works*. The Pelican Freud library vol. 14. Harmondsworth, Middlesex: Pelican Books.

Gergen, K. J. (1994) *Realities and relationships: Soundings in social constructionism*. Cambridge, Mass.: Harvard University Press.

Gersie, A. (1997) *Reflections on therapeutic story making: The use of stories in groups*. London: Jessica Kingsley.

Gordon, D. (1978) *Therapeutic metaphors*. Cupertino, Calif.: Metal.

Grainger, T. (1997) *Traditional storytelling: In the primary classroom*. Leamington Spa: Scholastic Ltd.

Gramling, L. F. & McCain, N. L. (1997) Grey glasses: Sadness in young women. *Journal of Advanced Nursing*, **26**, 312–19.

Grey, N., Young, K. & Holmes, E. (2002) Cognitive restructuring within reliving: A treatment for posttraumatic emotional hotspots in posttraumatic stress disorder. *Behavioural and Cognitive Psychotherapy*, **30**(1), 37–56.

Grice, H. P. (1975) Logic and conversation. In P. Cole & J. P. Morgan (Eds.). *Syntax and semantics 3: Speech acts*. New York: Academic Press.

Gross, H. S. (1995) Supportive therapy and the model of natural conversation. *Journal of Psychotherapy Practice and Research*, **4**(2), 182–3.

Gunn, D. M. & Fewell, D. N. (1993) *Narrative in the Hebrew Bible*. Oxford: Oxford University Press.

Guyatt, G. H., Sackett, D. L., Sinclair, J. C., Hayward, R., Cook, D. J. & Cook, R. J. (1995) Users' guides to the medical literature, IX ; A method for grading health care recommendations: Evidence based medicine working group. *Journal of the American Medical Association*, **274**, 1800–4.

Harrower, M. (1978) The therapy of poetry. In R. J. Rubin (Ed.). *Bibliotherapy sourcebook*. London: Oryx.

Hedberg, T. M. (1997) The re-enchantment of poetry as therapy. *The Arts in Psychotherapy*, **24**(1), 91–100.

Hinds, S. (1997) Once upon a time . . . therapeutic . . . stories as a psychiatric nursing intervention. *Journal of Psychosocial Nursing*, **35**(5), 46–7.

Holmes, J. (1995) Supportive psychotherapy: The search for positive meanings. *British Journal of Psychiatry*, **167**, 439–45.

Hynes, A. & Hynes-Berry, M. (1994) *Biblio/poetry therapy: The interactive process: A handbook*. St Cloud, Minn: North Star Press.

Jameson, F. (1972) *The prison-house of language*. Princeton, NJ: Princeton University Press.

Jensen, C. M. & Blair, S. F. E. (1997) Rhyme and reason in the relationship between creative writing and mental wellbeing. *British Journal of Occupational Therapy*, **60**(12), 525–30.

Jiranek, D. (2000) Use of hypnosis in pain management and post traumatic stress disorder. *Australian Journal of Clinical and Experimental Hypnosis*, **28**(2), 176–87.

Jones, A. (1997) Death, poetry, psychotherapy and clinical supervision. *Journal of Advanced Nursing*, **25**, 238–44.

Jones, A. & Buttrey, J. (1970) *Children and stories*. Oxford: Basil Blackwell.

Karantzis, N. & Lampropoulos, G. K. (2002) Reflecting on homework in psychotherapy: What can we conclude from research and experience? *Journal of Clinical Psychology*, **58**(5), 577–85.

Knights, B. (1995) *The listening reader: Fiction and poetry for counsellors and psychotherapists*. London and Bristol, Phil: Jessica Kingsley.

Kroger, W. S. & Fezler, W. D. (2002) Relaxing images in hypnobehavioural therapy. In A. A. Sheikh (Ed.). *Handbook of therapeutic imagery techniques: Imagery and human development series*. Amityville, NY: Baywood Publishing Company.

Labov, W. (1972) The transformation of experience in narrative syntax. In *Language in the inner city*. Philadelphia: University of Pennsylvania Press.

Labov, W. (1982) Speech actions and reactions in personal narrative. In D. Tannen (Ed.). *Georgetown round table in languages and linguistics*. Washington DC: Georgetown University Press.

Labov, W. & Waletzky, J. (1967) Narrative analysis: oral versions of personal experience. In J. Helm (Ed.). *Essays on the verbal and visual arts*. Seattle: University of Washington Press.

Lankton, C. H. & Lankton, S. R. (1989) *Tales of enchantment: Goal-oriented metaphors for adults and children in therapy*. New York: Brunner/Mazel.

Lazarus, A. (1971) *Behavior therapy and beyond*. New York: McGraw-Hill.

Lazarus, A. (1989) *The practice of multimodal therapy*. Baltimore, Md: Johns Hopkins University Press.

Lazarus, A. (1995) *Casebook of multimodal therapy*. New York: Guilford Press.

Leber, D. A. & Vanoli, E. G. (2001) Therapeutic use of humor: Occupational therapy clinicians' perceptions and practices. *American Journal of Occupational Therapy*, **55**(2), 221–6.

Lerner, A. (1975, September/October) Poetry as therapy. *American Psychological Association Monitor*, **9**(9–10), 4.

Lerner, A. (1981) Poetry therapy in the group experience. In R. J. Corsini (Ed.). *Handbook of innovative psychotherapies*. New York: Wiley.

Lerner, A. (Ed.)(1994) *Poetry in the therapeutic experience* (2nd edn). St Louis, Mo: MMB Music.

Lerner, A. (1996) Poetry therapy: A healing art. *Psychology and the Arts*, Spring/Summer, Division 10, The American Psychological Association.

Leuner, H. (1969) Guided affective imagery (GAI): A method of intensive psychotherapy. *American Journal of Psychotherapy*, **23**, 4–22.

Makari, G. J. & Shapiro, T. (1994) A linguistic model of psychotherapeutic listening. *Journal of Psychotherapy Practice and Research*, **3**(1), 37–43.

Marks, I. (2002) The maturing of therapy: Some brief psychotherapies help anxiety/depressive disorders but mechanisms of action are unclear. *British Journal of Psychiatry*, **180**(3), 200–4.

Martin, J., Cummings, A. & Hallberg, E. (1992) Therapists' intentional use of metaphor: Memorability, clinical impact, and possible epistemic/motivational functions. *Journal of Consulting and Clinical Psychology*, **60**, 143–5.

Mauer, M. H., Burnett, K., Ouellette, E. A., Ironson, G. H. & Dandes, H. M. (1999) Medical hypnosis and orthopaedic hand surgery: Pain perception, postoperative recovery and therapeutic comfort. *International Journal of Clinical and Experimental Hypnosis*, **47**(2), 144–61.

Mazza, N. (1993) Poetry therapy: Toward a research agenda for the 1990's. *Arts in Psychotherapy*, **20**, 51–9.

Mazza, N. (2003) *Poetry therapy: theory and practice*. New York: Routledge.

Mazza, N., Magaz, C. & Scaturoro, J. (1987) Poetry therapy with disturbed children. *The Arts in Psychotherapy*, **14**, 85–92.

McArdle, S. & Byrt, R. (2001) Fiction, poetry and mental health: Expressive and therapeutic uses of literature. *Journal of Psychiatric and Mental Health Nursing*, **8**, 517–24.

McCurry, S. & Hayes, S. (1992) Clinical and experimental perspectives on metaphorical talk. *Clinical Psychology Review*, **12**, 763–85.

McGibon, N. N. (1996) Writing as a therapeutic modality. *Journal of Psychosocial Nursing and Mental Health Services*, **34**(6), 31–5.

McLeod, J. (1997) *Narrative and psychotherapy*. London: Sage.

McMullin, R. E. (2000) *The new handbook of cognitive therapy techniques*. New York and London: W. W. Norton & Company.

McNamee, S. & Gergen, K. J. (1992) *Therapy as social construction*. London: Sage.

Mendlovic, S. & Doron, A. (2001) The 'story in a story' technique. *Contemporary Hypnosis*, **18**(2), 57–60.

Miller, D. N., Du Paul, G. J. & Lutz, J. G. (2002) School based psychosocial interventions for childhood depression: Acceptability of treatments among school psychologists. *School Psychology Quarterly*, **17**(1), 78–99.

Moller, A. T. & Steel, H. R. (2002) Clinically significant change after cognitive restructuring for adult survivors of childhood sexual abuse. *Journal of Rational-Emotive and Cognitive Behaviour Therapy*, **20**(1), 49–64.

Parry, A. (1991) A universe of stories. *Family Processes*, **30**, 37–54.

Parry, A. & Doan, R. E. (1994) *Story re-visions: Narrative therapy in the postmodern world*. New York: Guilford Press.

Pearce, S. S. (1996) *Flash of insight: Metaphor and narrative in therapy*. Boston, Mass.: Allyn & Bacon Inc.

Persons, J. B. & Miranda, J. (2002) Treating dysfunctional beliefs: Implications of the mood-state hypothesis. In R. L. Leahy & E. T. Dowd (Eds.). *Clinical advances in cognitive psychotherapy: Theory and application*. New York: Springer Publishing Co.

Polyani, L. (1978) *The American story: Cultural constraints on the structure and meaning of stories in conversation*. Unpublished doctoral thesis, University of Michigan.

Pratt, G. J., Wood, D. P. & Alman, B. M. (1988) *A clinical hypnosis primer*. Revised and expanded edition. New York: Wiley.

Pratt, M. L. (1977) *Toward a speech-act theory of literary discourse*. Bloomington: Indiana University Press.

Propp, V. (1968/1928) *The morphology of the folktale*. Austin: University of Texas.

Reissman, C. K. (1993a) *Narrative analysis*. Newbury Park, Calif.: Sage.

Reissman, C. K. (1993b) *Narrative analysis*, Qualitative Research Methods Series, 30. London: Sage.

Rennie, D. L. (1994) Storytelling in psychotherapy: The client's subjective experience. *Psychotherapy*, **31**(2), 234–43.

Reynolds, S. (2000) Evidence based practice and psychotherapy research. *Journal of Mental Health*, **9**(3), 257–66.

Ricoeur, P. (1977) *The rule of metaphor: Multi-disciplinary studies of the creation of meaning in language* (trans. R. Czerny, K. McLaughlin & J. Costello). Toronto: University of Toronto Press.

Ricoeur, P. (1991) Life quest of narrative. In D. Wood (Ed.). *On Paul Ricouer: Narrative and interpretation*. London: Routledge.

Ricoeur, P. (1997) *From text to action*. Chicago: Northwestern University Press.

Rosen, S. (1982) *My voice will go with you: The teaching tales of Milton H. Erickson*. London: Norton.

Rosenwald, G. C. & Ochberg, R. L. (1992) *Storied lives: The cultural politics of self understanding*. New Haven: Yale University Press.

Rossiter, C. (1996) Review of bruise theory. *Journal of Poetry Therapy*, **9**(3), 167–9.

Sackett, D. L., Richardson, W. S., Rosenberg, W. & Haynes, R. B. (1997) *Evidence based medicine: How to practice and teach EBM*. New York: Churchill Livingstone.

Saleebey, D. (1994) Culture, theory and narrative: The intersection of meanings in practice. *Social Work*, **39**, 351.

Sanderson, W. C. & McGinn, L. K. (2001) Cognitive behavioural therapy of depression. In M. N. Weissman (Ed.). *Treatment of depression: Bridging the 21st century*. New York: American Psychopathological Association.

Sarbin, T. R. (Ed.)(1986) *Narrative psychology: The storied nature of human conduct*. New York: Praeger.

Sarbin, T. (1990) Metaphors of unwanted conduct: a historical sketch. In D. E. Leary (Ed.). *Metaphors in the history of psychology*. New York: Cambridge University Press.

Sawyer, R. (1942) *The way of the storyteller*. New York: The Viking Press.

Schoenberger, N. E., Kirsch, I., Gearan, P. & Montgomery, G. (1997) Hypnotic enhancement of a cognitive behavioural treatment for public speaking anxiety. *Behaviour Therapy*, **28**(1), 127–40.

Scholes, R. & Kellogg, R. (1966) *The nature of narrative*. New York: Oxford University Press.

Searle, J. (1969) *Speech acts: An essay in the philosophy of language*. London: Cambridge University Press.

Sheikh, A. (Ed.)(1983a) *Imagery: Current theory, research and application*. New York: Wiley.

Sheikh, A. (Ed.)(1983b) *Imagination and healing*. New York: Baywood.

Sheikh, A. & Shaffer, J. (Eds.)(1979) *The potential of fantasy and imagination*. New York: Brandon House.

Shorr, J. (1972) *Psycho-imagination therapy: The integration of phenomenology and imagination*. New York: Intercontinental.

Shorr, J. (1974) *Psychotherapy through imagery*. New York: Intercontinental.

Siegelman, E. (1990) *Metaphor and meaning in psychotherapy*. New York: Guilford Press.

Singer, J. (1974) *Imagery and daydream methods in psychotherapy and behaviour modification*. New York: Academic Press.

Singer, J. (1976) *Daydreaming and fantasy*. London: Allen & Unwin.

Singer, J. (Ed.)(1995) *Repression and dissociation: Implications for personality theory, psychopathology and health*. Chicago: University of Chicago Press.

Singer, J. & Pope, K. (Eds.)(1978) *The power of human imagination*. New York: Plenum.

Smith, C. & Nylund, D. (Eds.)(1997) *Narrative therapies with children and adolescents*. New York: Guilford Press.

Smucker, M. R., Danu, C., Foa, E. B. & Niederee, J. L. (2002) Imagery re-scripting: A new treatment for survivors of childhood sexual abuse suffering from posttraumatic stress. In R. L. Leahy & E. T. Dowd (Eds.). *Clinical advances in cognitive psychotherapy: Theory and applications*. New York: Springer Publishing Co.

Sperry, R. (1968) Hemispheric disconnection and unity of conscious awareness. *American Psychologist*, **23**, 723–33.

Stubbs, M. (1983) On speaking terms: Inspecting conversational data. In *Discourse analysis: The sociolinguistic analysis of natural language*. Oxford: Basil Blackwell.

Tannen, D. (1979) 'What's in a frame?'. In R. Freedle (Ed.). *New directions in discourse processing*. Norwood, NJ: Ablex.

Tomkins, M. A. (2002) Guidelines for enhancing homework compliance. *Journal of Clinical Psychology*, **58**(5), 565–76.

Toolan, M. (1988) Narrative as socially situated: The sociolinguistic approach. In *Narrative: A Critical Linguistic Introduction*. London: Routledge & Kegan Paul.

Tooze, R. (1959) *Storytelling*. Englewood Cliffs, NJ: Prentice-Hall Inc.

Watzlawick, P. (1978) *The language of change*. New York: Brunner/Mazel.

Wenckus, E. M. (1994) Storytelling: Using an ancient art to work with groups. *Journal of Psychosocial Nursing and Mental Health Services*, **32**(7), 30–2.

White, M. & Epston, D. (1990) *Narrative means to therapeutic ends*. New York: Sage.

Wright, A. (1995) *Storytelling with children*. Oxford: Oxford University Press.

Zarren, J. & Eimer, B. (2002) *Brief cognitive hypnosis: Facilitating the change of dysfunctional behaviour*. New York: Springer Publishing Co.

Zeig, J. K. (Ed.)(1980) *A teaching seminar with Milton H. Erickson*. New York: Brunner/Mazel.

Zeig, J. K. & Gilligan, S. (Eds.)(1990) *Brief therapy: Myths, methods and metaphors*. Brunner/Mazel.

Zimmerman, J. L. & Dickerson, V. C. (1996) *If problems talked: Narrative therapy in action* (The Guilford Family Therapy Series). New York: Guilford Press.

2 ATTITUDE SHIFT

At the heart of improving the way that individuals think about themselves and their emotions, behaviour or self image is attitude change. In therapeutic storytelling, to change people's response to negative emotions, behaviour or self image, attitude change or shift will be fundamental. In this chapter, we outline what is meant by 'attitude shift', before looking, in subsequent chapters, at how this can be achieved in our three core territories or domains of emotions, behaviour and self image. The term 'attitude' is familiar to anyone who has ever studied psychology. Forming attitudes, changing them and re-tuning them to suit changed circumstances are probably among the oldest of human social crafts. For example, the use of stories and storytelling techniques was certainly an important part of the rhetoric of classical orators and politicians in ancient Greece and Rome, and the arts of rhetoric were an important part of the education of young gentlemen in Europe through the Middle Ages and Renaissance. However, in the present day, this skill features little in the training of psychotherapists and counsellors. In this chapter we will be attempting to demonstrate how storytelling in therapy may be rediscovered in relation to attitude shift and explain how the literature on attitudes may be mobilised to make us more skilled therapeutic communicators. We will also attempt to describe some stories, which we have found useful in promoting attitude change and ameliorating clients' distress.

The notion of attitude change is pervasive in therapy. From Freud's seminal notion that he sought to turn neuroses into everyday worries through to contemporary concerns with cognitive restructuring, therapists have sought to make the sources of clients' distress more easily tackled and less scary. In therapy, stories can have a prime role inasmuch as they may help encourage a more adaptive perspective on life.

We will not concern ourselves with a detailed definition of attitudes here, as this is well rehearsed in most introductory psychology books. A brief definition, therefore, will suffice. McGuire (1985, p. 239) says that attitudes are 'responses that locate objects of thought on dimensions of judgement'. The objects of thought may be issues, people or items about which participants have an opinion. 'Dimensions of judgement' refers to the range over which evaluations extend, good to bad, from dirty to clean, from nice to nasty and so on. Ajzen (1982) defines them more briefly as 'predispositions to act in a certain way'. In contrast to attitudes, the related notion of values is a little different. Values are broad abstract goals that lack a specific object or reference point, for example, bravery, beauty or freedom. A further related notion is that of opinion, which is a less easily defined term relating to attitudes and often refers to the shared (or divided) attitudes of groups of people or nations, as in 'public opinion'. For our discussion here it is important to distinguish three major aspects or components of attitudes.

First there is a cognitive component, relating to beliefs, ideas and knowledge. Second, there is an affective component involving emotional aspects, for example, liking, respect, sympathy, contempt, fear and revulsion. Third, there is a behavioural component, which involves tendencies towards action. The three components do not always match in any simple way. Two people may share the belief that, say, human existence is futile, yet one may be distressed about it and the other may find such a realisation liberating. People may share the belief that computers are useful but have very different emotional feelings about them and differ in their willingness to use them.

In the last 50 years or so of work on attitude change in social psychology and communication studies the role of stories has been under-emphasised. Nevertheless, from the early studies of Carl Hovland and his colleagues at Yale, there were important aspects of storytelling in the messages. Hovland's wartime job was to help persuade American servicemen that it was a good thing to fight in World War 2 in Europe. On the face of it he had an uphill struggle. Young men had to be persuaded that it was desirable to be stationed in the UK, a country where the locals were hostile ('overpaid, oversexed and over here' was an English description of American troops), and fly life-threatening missions over German-controlled territory. Hovland and his colleagues studied the effect of film maker Frank Capra's classic 'Why we fight' series of films (Hovland et al., 1953). The engaging documentary style and storytelling skills of Capra were certainly effective. The troops learned a great deal – far more than from conventional lectures - but Hovland discovered that it was much more difficult to get them to feel differently about the war. They were no more enthusiastic about dying for their country.

Despite the apparent differences between wartime propaganda and therapeutic attitude change, there are lessons to be learned for the therapeutic storyteller in much of this work, in terms of how we present the story, the order of the message, the source it appears to come from and the kinds of characters we populate it with. That is, a message may be more believable if the source appears similar to the recipients, if the source appears not to be speaking out of self interest, and messages containing both sides of the argument are more effective if the audience is initially sceptical of the communicator's point of view. These kinds of findings can aid us in structuring messages or stories. Hovland also introduced the idea of a 'sleeper effect' – that a message may become more effective over time, even after important details are forgotten. According to more recent research by Priester et al. (1999) the sleeper effect is more likely to occur if the initial presentation of the message is more detailed and elaborate. In other words, more like a story.

Social psychology was interested in cognition well before researchers elsewhere in the discipline had caught on. Social psychologists were researching how people make inferences, how attitudes change and how people resolve contradictions in their thinking around the time that much of the work was being done by Ellis and Beck that laid the foundations for cognitive behavioural therapy as we know it today.

It is a fundamental premise of both social psychology and cognitive behavioural therapy that attitudes help us filter and organise our experience. They serve as a template with which to compare incoming data. The idea of using attitude change as a way of reducing the negative impact of adverse events, however, goes back even earlier. The Stoic philosopher Epictetus said 'Men are disturbed not by things but by the view that they take of them'. Lankton and Lankton (1989, p. 69) remind us that attitudes may influence perception. Attitudes are the templates that 'reduce the incoming sensory data to a subset that is consistent with the ideas previously held'. To put the situation very simply, the assumption is that the attitudes of a depressed, stressed or anxious person act as a kind of filter so that information that conforms to their negative view of themselves is given disproportionate importance. There may be biases in attention, memory retrieval and in the processing structures that are activated. This self confirming bias means that information that disconfirms or challenges an attitude may not usually be perceived, due to the filtering and framing process involved in holding the attitude. Moreover, a good deal of this becomes automatic over the course of a person's lifetime so that the negative and self punishing habits of thought will contribute to the person's depression or anxiety, without them realising quite why it happens. It becomes part of the person's unquestioned 'common sense' about themselves or their situation. In Beck's original formulation (e.g. Beck, 1967; 1991) the attitudes of a person undergoing depression originate in childhood, perhaps involving them internalising injunctions such as 'I must succeed or no one will love me'. As Beck himself points out, many failures are inevitable in a full and active life, so there are many opportunities for such attitudes to be reinforced. In depression, Beck believes that a client's thinking forms a 'cognitive triad' characterised by a negative view of their experiences, themselves and their futures. Despite the fact that this condition is often unpleasant, it has a reassuring predictability to it, which clients may be unwilling to disrupt.

Once a negative pattern of attitudes and thinking has been established it may be difficult for a therapist to change this for a variety of reasons. First, there may be a 'confirmatory bias' in thinking, as we have mentioned earlier. A client with a sense of failure may well feel that they have failed the therapist as well, if progress appears to be slow. Unfolding events are interpreted in line with the existing schema. A second reason why the belief and attitude system in distressed clients may be difficult to change is to do with resistance (Beutler et al., 2001). For example, a challenge to an attitude is often perceived as some sort of threat and consequently calls defensive measures into play. Clients may also be resistant to change, even after they have recognised the mistaken quality of maladaptive beliefs, because they do not see the promise in the alternatives presented by the therapist (Rasmussen, 2002). Moreover, the resistance may be bolstered by what Rasmussen (p. 148) describes as 'fear of worthlessness and lack of courage to be imperfect'.

The idea of attitudes then can help us see what is wrong with the information processing of people in therapy for anxiety disorders or depression. If we can change them, perhaps with the right kind of story, then the client will leave the therapy room revitalised, ready to tackle life's disappointments with renewed vigour. Unfortunately our approach in this book has no such predictable certainty. The notion of attitudes as it was once upon a time conceived in social psychology and in Beck's original account of cognitive factors in therapy has been challenged by a variety of new social psychologies that have sprung up in the last 20 years. Scholars have been increasingly informed by the tenets of postmodernism, social constructionism and discourse analysis, which have led them to reformulate what attitudes mean. Therefore, without undertaking a long and complex detour through these intellectual movements, let us briefly try to arrive at a definition of what we are talking about that is sensitive both to the tasks of the therapist and to the new intellectual movements that have made their home in psychology. One notion that could intersect with both older notions of 'attitude' and with newer, social constructionist psychologies comes from the philosopher Hans Georg Gadamer (1960). One of Gadamer's notions, reminiscent of both early notions of attitudes and later ideas about constructionism, is his emphasis on the 'horizon of understanding', which the reader inevitably brings to the text. By extension, this applies to human attempts to interpret any events. As Gadamer argues, all readings must necessarily flow from what he calls this forestructure of understanding – what it is the reader presumes about the world, the people in it, the rules by which it works. Sense making must inevitably take place within this horizon. Drawing from literary theory also, a similar argument is made by a number of other scholars of literature and communication. As Stanley Fish (1980), Janice Radway (1984), Thomas Lindlof (1988) and Kenneth Gergen (1994; 1997) have argued, every reader – or any other kind of sense maker - is a member of some interpretive community, a network of people who understand the world in certain ways. Whatever interpretation of social reality they make, it must fall back on these understandings or forestructures.

Whereas we have called this chapter 'attitude shift', as changing attitudes has historically been an important part of therapy, we want to highlight also how human beings are embedded in storytelling and interpretive practice. Sometimes it is not entirely clear cut what the difference is between an attitude, a story, a metaphor or a 'forestructure'. Moreover, as most human understanding takes place using concepts, languages and emotions, which are intelligible not just to one person but a whole community, it is sometimes not entirely clear where an attitude has come from, or what a client is trying to do by expressing such a thing.

This blending of attitude, image and metaphor can be illustrated by a participant in Gramling and McCain's (1997) study of sadness in young women to describe a negative, self confirming mindset as that of 'grey glasses': 'It's like people say Pollyanna looks through rose coloured glasses, well it's like my glasses are grey' (p. 315). Usually there is a great deal of information available to 'prove' that the negative attitudes are 'true'. The conventional view then, would perhaps point to the way that a depressed person may be able to demonstrate readily that 'nobody cares' as every postponed visit, late phone call and missed birthday can quickly be taken as evidence of this. Thus, attitudes act as filters that gather evidence, which, in turn, tautologically tends to support the premises on which the attitude is based. Indeed, if a therapist tries to challenge or dispute the client's attitudes then this too can be taken as evidence that the therapist does not really care or cannot possibly understand the burden under which the client is labouring. The constructionist and postmodernist movement might also point to the way that the 'grey glasses' quote involves allusions to well-known metaphors and stories, which are part of the wisdom of our particular interpretive community and are recognisable ways of making sense of the mind.

This complexity means that an approach to dealing with distress that relies on stories is particularly apt. Structures of attitudes looked at in this way are considerably more than dimensions of judgement, and their very embeddedness in cultural commonplaces means that they are difficult to shift. This situation is one where indirect approaches such as using stories or anecdotes might be particularly valuable as they do not involve confrontation. Strong (2002) suggests that therapists' ability to engage with clients in their own discursive terms is particularly crucial, a point echoed by Jenkins (2001), who argues that talking about matters of interest to the client is valuable. It is disarming, 'cuts through resistance' (p. 46) and renders the healing process enjoyable, especially where the therapist is able to mobilise the kinds of metaphors that are appealing to the client. Thus, to optimise the likely attitude change, stories should be ones the client can identify with and should in a sense bridge the client's old and new attitude.

Even when we acknowledge the socialised complexity of clients' attitudes, notions from the psychology of attitude change are still useful. The negative attitudes that cognitive therapists believe underlie the depressive and anxiety disorders may not yield to direct challenge, but there are other ways of making headway. One way of explaining this is to think of attitudes as needing constant reinforcement in order to stay the same. Many of us can remember learning about behaviourism and the idea of operant conditioning, where the 'organism' repeats actions that are reinforcing. Negative attitudes are 'reinforced' frequently – rather like the 'continuous reinforcement schedule' in operant conditioning research. Thus, the hope is that when they are not reinforced, they will extinguish quite quickly, rather like the rat that gives up pressing the lever when it no longer dispenses the food pellet every time.

That, then, is the theory. However, often clients are firmly entrenched in such beliefs and likely to dismiss, discount and discredit evidence to the contrary. Therefore, indirect, metaphorical and allegorical modalities may allow a person to gently consider and think about a different belief system. They may be able to imagine how a new belief system would support new relational patterns that would not adequately be addressed by the old. Attitude change, therefore, has a dual focus. One element of it is designed to match, encourage identification with and then shed doubt on the existing attitude. The other element illustrates the more advantageous attitude, which is the therapeutic goal, and its consequences in action.

Pursuing this line of argument, we could even press on as far as Kenneth

Gergen when he says that life and language themselves are forms of play. This offers the possibility that '... we might play with the truths of the day, shake them about, try them on like funny hats. Serious concerns are left at the carnival gate' (Gergen, 1991, p. 189). As well as changing attitudes per se, the stories with which clients are presented represent opportunities for '... multiple and disparate potentials for being' (Gergen, 1991, p. 69). The repertoire of stories told by therapists in their daily work with clients '... not only opens relationships to new ranges of possibility but one's subjective life also becomes more fully laminated' (Gergen, 1991, p. 71), 'laminated' in this context presumably meaning more richly layered, so that there are more possibilities for clients to choose between.

It is not always possible to change all the elements of an attitude at once. As noted above, over half a century ago, Hovland's American troops learned more about the war, but were no more enthusiastic about dying in it. In the same way, any therapists have noted with frustration that they can discuss maladaptive attitudes with clients, yet emotional and behavioural changes are much more difficult to accomplish (Kinney, 2000; Hauck, 2001). Guilt especially has been identified as being very resistant to change (Eagle, 1999; Walkerdine et al., 2001), and persists after other social and psychological changes have been accomplished.

In order to have a chance of accomplishing attitude change, then, it is important that the story fits the client. From the earliest studies of attitude change, it appears that the messages that are most effective are those that are most easily fitted in with what the receiver already knows, feels or believes (Jowett & O'Donnell, 1992). Factors such as the perceived similarity between the receiver and the source, the prestige of the source and whether the source seems to be advocating a position contrary to his or her interests all seem to be relevant. Allied to this, some researchers and commentators have noted that change is most readily accomplished if the message addresses something that the receiver is not really committed to. John Naisbitt (1982, p. 91) said in *Megatrends*: 'When people really care about an issue, it doesn't matter how much is spent to influence their vote, they will go with their beliefs. When an issue is inconsequential to the voters, buying their vote is a snap.' Stories as vehicles for attitude change, then, have the virtue of appearing peripheral (they are, after all, usually about someone or something else), yet at the same time, if they are well chosen, can be relevant, credible and applicable to the client's situation.

The advantage of encapsulating the attitude change message in a story – even if it is apparently about something else – is clear from a study by Lee and Leets (2002) who discovered that implicit messages within well-developed narrative structures were more effective in political persuasion than explicit messages within simplistic narrative structures. The obviously didactic narrative, in other words, was much less persuasive. Thus we see the importance of using stories that carry implicit messages when attempting to change client attitudes.

To understand how to make stories effective in therapy it is useful to borrow an idea from music therapy called the 'isoprinciple' (Leedy, 1985; Reed, 1999).

This involves selecting the work of music or poetry that 'not only matches the feelings and perceptions of the client, but balances that feeling with others, always opening to a larger recognition of truth, a more wholesome balance among feelings, such as a movement from despair to hope' (Reed, 1999, p. 103).

There are other techniques to make the story fit the client and enhance the attitude changing effect it might have. In making sense of the clients we encounter and tailoring the stories to them, it is of course desirable to make sure the stories resonate with the client's experience and situation. Let us try to be a little more specific about some of the techniques in use. One of the areas where this has reached a fine art is not in therapy, but in the arena of so called psychic readings and the sorts of stage shows that are performed by mediums who form a popular part of US daytime television. Without going into the complex theological debates surrounding the possible survival of the soul after death, or the likelihood of contacting the spirit of a departed relative, there are some important social psychological insights for the therapist to be gained from this ancient craft. We are not advocating that therapists act as fairground shysters. However, it is possible to use this framework as a guide for creating a more therapeutically engaging practice that interlocks convincingly with clients' experiences. Generally, the practitioners' folk wisdom divides this process up into three kinds of 'reading', known as cold reading, warm reading and hot reading techniques.

1. **Cold reading.** In this variant, the therapeutic storyteller, like the stage mentalist or the medium, does not do the reading and the clients help the professional out a great deal. The professional asks them questions and they give him or her answers. A stage medium might say 'I'm getting a B name. Who could this be?', 'I'm seeing someone in uniform. Who is this please?'. And so on. This technique can be adapted to therapeutic ends in working with a client about whom we know very little, where you 'read' someone 'cold', knowing nothing about them. To tailor the therapeutic session or story to the client, one might commence by asking lots of questions and making numerous statements, some general and some specific. This will enable us to see what 'sticks'. This can be detected in terms of verbal agreement, but many stage practitioners are sensitive to nonverbal cues too. Some of these may seem counterintuitive – for example, where clients nod their heads this may well indicate disagreement. Again, like the stage performer cold reading, this may yield a good many mistakes and dead ends, but in the same way it is only necessary to secure the occasional 'hit' to make progress and to enlist the client into the process.
2. **Warm reading.** This uses some of our everyday and professional knowledge about people to make inferences. For example, the stage practitioner may shrewdly believe that most bereaved people will wear a piece of jewellery that connects them to their loved one. The practitioner may say 'Do you have a ring or a piece of jewellery on you by any chance?'. The client of the magician or stage psychic may be amazed at the acuity. Whereas to the stage

practitioner this can be a way of making the act look convincing, in therapeutic contexts the practitioner might use the same insight to alert themselves to the applicability of stories of keepsakes, mementoes, remembrances, photographs on bedside tables and so on.

3. **Hot reading.** Sceptics often allege that stage mentalists or mediums cheat by obtaining information on their subjects ahead of the show. There are allegations that practitioners may use concealed microphones in waiting areas, confederates in the audience, search through refuse, plunder newspaper files to obtain information on celebrity clients and 'pump' friends or relatives for useful snippets of information. Whereas some of these techniques may be illegal, unethical and often wholly beyond the resources of the average mental health practitioner, there is still a great deal of collateral information that can be used to ensure that the stories used fit the client. Records, letters of referral and insights from colleagues, friends and relatives may provide some clues as to the applicability of a story.

Once we have some clues as to the kinds of stories and issues that might appeal to the client and might enable some therapeutic change, it is important to try to establish the kinds of changes that it would be most appropriate to make. Historically, of course, cognitive behaviour therapy has pioneered the technique of deciding with the client the kinds of changes they would like to make and discussing agendas for the therapy. Equally, it may be that change is thwarted by some sets of attitudes held by the client. It is often the case in therapy that certain attitudes, for example, the attitude that 'no one cares', prevent the client from changing their lives for the better. Any governing attitude can act like a self-fulfilling prophecy, maintaining or even increasing the distress clients suffer. Clients may play the detective and seek out evidence to 'prove' that these attitudes are true. Thus the depressed person may be able to 'prove' that no one cares and thus remains in thrall to that attitude. Such an attitude may be so strong that even more objective evidence may fail to change it. In a sense, the client-detective will resist the counter evidence of the therapist-detective. Here, the indirect use of well-chosen metaphors may get under the client's radar and effect gentle change. The use of detective or research skills may be harnessed by the therapist in other ways too. Burns (1999) gives the example of a young man who was distressed at what he saw to be the high level of conflict in his marriage. With the therapist's encouragement, he was induced to ask friends and acquaintances – especially those who seemed to have happy marriages – whether they had any experience of marital conflict. His mini survey taught him that not only was such conflict remarkably common, but also that many people didn't seem to see anything wrong with it. Of course, we are not seeking to trivialise marital conflict or domestic violence, but to point out that the sense of being 'the only one' can be distressing and that detective work by the client can be reconfigured so as to yield less distress rather than more.

Despite the use of stories to offer a relatively gentle format for attitude change, there are many therapeutic activities that might involve presenting a challenge to a client. There are a variety of ways in which we might offer challenges politely in everyday speech, perhaps by hedging or qualifying our comments, for example, 'some people might think ...' or 'just for the sake of argument ...', and deploying these therapeutically. In a sense, then, most of us are already skilled in dressing up potentially unpalatable information in the form of a 'story' of sorts. Sometimes the client may be asked to challenge them him or herself. This can be done in the form of role play, when clients are invited to play the role of a particularly critical other. Alternatively, for clients who are prone to feel foolish or ashamed when doing something in front of other people, therapists sometimes recommend 'shame attacking exercises'. An example might be shouting out the name of stops on the tube or bus and noting that the consequences are not catastrophic (Burns, 1999). There are stories of therapists vying with each other to challenge their own tendencies towards shame. A legend, which Burns ascribes to one of Albert Ellis's colleagues, depicts the therapist walking into an American 'drugstore' and asking loudly for condoms. When asked what kind he wanted, he replied, 'Do you have any extra teensy weensy sized ones?'. Clearly, exercises designed to challenge clients' social fears need not always be so taxing, but this story may be used to make homework exercises such as saying hello to strangers seem less daunting, and even make homework fun, as a source of amusing anecdotes that can be shared later.

As well as short and humorous anecdotes to oil the wheels of the therapeutic process we have discovered that there is also a role for more extended allegorical tales in helping attitude change and encouraging clients to take a more flexible approach in solving problems and changing attitudes. This relies on the premise that one way of encouraging attitude shift may be to present a story that offers little room for negotiation or considering other perspectives to stimulate thoughts about what could have been done differently. For instance, consider the following story retold by Gersie (1997), adapted from Shah (1979). This story follows a common pattern of stories with a 'trouble' of some kind at its heart. Such stories contribute to their usefulness in therapy or education because difficulties in the management of conflict are often the core of a client's problems:

THE OPEN DOOR

A newly married couple arrive in their new home. It is a dark and stormy night. Just as they are about to snuggle into bed, they hear the sound of a door flapping in the wind. They realise that in their hurry to carry the wedding gifts safely indoors, they must have forgotten to shut the door. The groom says to the bride: 'The door has been left open hasn't it?'. When she asks him to close it, he replies in anger: 'Me? Why should I? Can't you go and do it yourself?'. She refuses. They haggle, urge and accuse one another for a while, but to no avail. Neither of them wants to go downstairs and close the front door. However, as this is their first wedding night, they decide that they must find a solution to their problem. They agree to stay in the room, go to bed and to keep silent. The first one to speak will have to go downstairs to close the front door. They believe that their wager of silence will only last a little while. One of them surely will say something to end this hassle. But they grossly underestimate the other's stubbornness. They lie there next to each other, eyes closed, determined not to speak. They bring to their battle of wills all the defiance and commitment they can muster.

Well, as it is a dark and stormy night, the flapping door has been noticed by thieves who are doing their rounds. Under the cover of night they creep into the house and take whatever wedding gifts they can lay their hands on. As the couple are still awake, trying their very best not to be the loser of the wager of silence, they even hear the thieves wander round the house. But still, they manage not to speak. In this way they spend their first wedding night, neither succumbing to the other's will.

When daylight comes disquieted neighbours notice that the front door of the newly wedded couple's house is wide open. They talk about what to do. At last they decide that they must go into the house. Stunned at the havoc the thieves have wrought, they knock at last on the bedroom door. There is no reply. Terrified at the thought of what might have happened to the couple, they open the door. To their horror they see the newly weds sitting upright in bed. They look proudly defiant and still refuse to speak. Whatever the neighbours do, they can't get them to talk. In exasperation one of them shakes the man by the shoulders and shouts 'Talk, talk'. The young woman cries: 'Please, don't hurt him.' Triumphantly the husband croons: 'I won! I won. You have to shut the door.'

What can we deduce from this story? That people become concerned with trivia at the expense of maintaining a focus on more important things? That people may be overly concerned with their place in hierarchies or have a sense that it is unjust for them to have to change when they feel it is others who have initiated the problem? Getting clients to think about how to solve this problem can help to illustrate a number of cognitive behavioural techniques, for example, a technique based on cost benefit analysis, where clients are encouraged to think of the advantages and disadvantages of a piece of dysfunctional thinking or behaviour and rate each of them. The hope is that with a situation like this, the disadvantages of the protagonist's behaviour will outweigh the advantages. Moreover, it can be used to illustrate the difficulties that 'all or nothing thinking' can lead to, as well as being overly caught up with 'should statements' – about what the other person 'should' do – or blame. His story also alludes to some of the tenets of anger management therapy. An important part of anger is the way it involves some sort of demand – for fairness, respect, agreement, willingness to do things the way the protagonist prefers and so on. Whereas the lack of these things is disappointing, in angry people this disappointment readily translates into anger. Part of the cognitive restructuring that is sometimes suggested is that these demands that lie at the heart of anger should be redefined as desires. Saying 'I would like' something means that problems on the pathway to fulfilment are more easily resolved.

The classic conception of clients' attitudes in cognitive behavioural therapy is that they provide relatively enduring rules for life. Further, these attitudes can sometimes be unhelpful to us. Beck's original intimation that the client's attitudes hold the key to the anxiety or depression they suffer from led him to develop the 'dysfunctional attitude scale' (Weissman & Beck, 1979). This questionnaire aims to measure what he called the 'silent postulates', which in his view form the basis of the cognitive triad of depressive attitudes. The dysfunctional attitude scale addresses seven domains of attitude from which depression appeared to originate, namely approbation, love, success, perfectionism, allowing oneself rights, demands or obligations, omnipotence, and autonomy, measured by means of the participant's agreement with 40 items (Weissman & Beck, 1979; Legeron, 1997). To give a flavour of the scale, here are some typical items:

 4 If I do not do well all the time, people will not respect me.
11 If I can't do something well there is no point in trying.
16 I am nothing if a person I love doesn't love me.
23 I should be upset if I made a mistake.

In Beck's formulation, a high degree of agreement with statements like this will tend to be associated with depression. Indeed, this prediction has been borne out by research, in that depressed people are indeed more likely to agree with the statements (Weintraub et al., 1974; Furlong & Oei, 2002). However, cognitive content alone does not invariably cause sorrowful emotion, and dysfunctional attitudes are not specific to depression. The implication of much of this work, though, is that while there is not an inevitable correspondence between these variables, it is nevertheless beneficial to a person's mood to tackle the overly self critical attitudes of the kind measured on the dysfunctional attitude scale.

In a good deal of therapy, which draws on the cognitive behavioural tradition, therapists proceed along the lines of the so called ABC model. As we discussed briefly in chapter 1, this widely used approach involves a causal scenario for distressing emotions, which contains three elements, namely an activating event (A), the automatic thoughts, reflexive reactions or dysfunctional attitudes and beliefs (B), which are activated, and the upsetting emotional consequences (C). In this view, an important part of the therapy is to familiarise clients with this model and, instead of allowing themselves to be controlled by the automatic thoughts (B), the therapist introduces disputation (D). If we imagine a person who has recently come out of a long-term relationship, part of their distress may relate to automatic thoughts and silent postulates such as 'No one will ever love me again', 'I'm a failure at relationships' or 'I'll spend the rest of my life alone'. The task of the therapist, according to this model, would be to dispute these beliefs and suggest to the protagonist perhaps that they can make a difference by concentrating on having high quality relationships with the people around him or her, developing a satisfying social life, concentrating on fulfilment from work, or establishing that the client's success in romantic relationships in the future will be determined by the effort he or she makes.

However, some clients maintain that certain antecedents, such as traumatic childhood experiences or hereditary factors, override the effects of any percep- tion or thought. In addition there are political understandings of our position as part of a class, gender or racialised hierarchy and the way this may disadvantage some groups of people. As the saying of the 1970s had it, you can't just think your way out of oppression. Whereas all these factors lead to challenges for the individual and the community, one of the valuable contributions that storytelling therapy can make is that it can help to challenge the 'myths of inevitability', which accompany some kinds of distress. For example the great nineteenth-century psychiatrist Richard Von Krafft-Ebing (1886) describes how his patients often struggled with their urge to masturbate. He, and they, believed that this originated as a hereditary problem, for example, as a result of coming from a 'tainted family'. Moreover, if the patient succumbed to these urges, he risked further neurological damage, beginning with 'spinal irritation' and ending, inevitably, with insanity and death. The fear that this had for people in nineteenth-century Europe is perhaps difficult to imagine now; the hereditary inevitability of yesteryear has become obsolete as a result of changes in social norms and values around sexuality.

The myths of inevitability often spill over into a client's thinking about the nature of their problems and the difficulty of changing anything for the better. Antecedents may incline a person to think or act a certain way but do not necessarily force them. Indeed, the negative circumstances may be transformed into something creative. Arthur Frank and John Diamond have advanced our knowledge of what it is like to have cancer by means of their accounts of their illnesses (Frank, 1995; 1997; 1998; Diamond, 1999), and David Karp has informed us of what it is like to suffer from depression and hope for relief from medication (Karp, 1992; 1993). Even physiological experiences like having operations and taking medications are lurid with meaning and are subject to interpretation and evaluation which present numerous points of contact for therapists to grasp. Even in dire cases, such as when a patient is dying, therapists can mitigate or offset the client's concerns about their impending demise (Leyden-Rubenstein, 2001). Even when dealing with the most profound horrors of recent history, it is possible to address the cognitive processes of attaching meanings to events and how these meanings trigger emotions. This is aptly illustrated by considering the ways in which therapists and clients are still trying to come to terms with the Nazi Holocaust of the 1930s and 1940s. McMullin (2000, p. 24) describes the case of Anna who presented with generalised anxiety and depression. As a child, before World War 2, the Germans invaded the Russian village where she lived. The inhabitants were enslaved and eventually lined up and machined gunned to fall into a gully. Anna was pushed under the falling bodies and shielded from the bullets. She remained under the bodies all night, too frightened to move, and was found by neighbouring villagers the next morning. She was the only survivor.

As therapy couldn't change what had happened the focus had to be on changing how she viewed it. The therapist focused on her beliefs rather than the event and gradually she learned to accept what had happened. She learned that 'the universe isn't the way she would like it to be. It can be nasty and painful, and it has no obligation to be different from what it is'. When she accepted living in this kind of universe her anxiety and depression alleviated. This kind of work, in dealing with the mass human tragedies of recent history is being carried on by a number of workers (e.g. Maoz & Bar-On, 2002), who describe a storytelling approach to help build peace and reconciliation between historically opposed groups. No matter how horrific the early experiences, there are therapists who attempt to enable clients to rise above all these and free themselves by changing the way they look at life.

This kind of logic also applies to people overcoming disabilities. Many of us are familiar from our schooldays with the story of Helen Keller, born in America in 1880, and left blind and deaf at the age of two by a childhood illness. With the help of her parents and with a dedicated teacher, 'Miss Sullivan', she gradually acquired language skills. Whereas this was considered remarkable in itself, the part of the story that we were never told at school is that Helen went on to gain fame as an activist for causes such as disability rights, trade unionism, feminism and the welfare of people disabled in World War 2. She listed Lenin as one of her heroes and was considered sufficiently subversive for the FBI to accumulate a substantial file on her. Whereas it is difficult for us to know exactly what 'cognitive restructuring' this would have involved, the important feature of this case is that it is possible to triumph over these kinds of adversities.

Thus, given the benefits of cognitive restructuring, it is not surprising that therapists have devoted some considerable time and effort to making sense of how it can be done. As McMullin (2000) indicates, the role for stories within cognitive restructuring is to help clients assume a more adaptive perspective on their lives. McMullin proposes two essential requirements for the use of this technique. These relate to the relevance of the story for each client and also ensuring that the story demonstrates a bridge between the client's old or existing belief and a new, more helpful belief.

McMullin prescribes a method for doing this:

1. Synthesize the client's core beliefs into a story. Each story should consist of the major situations the client has faced, the major emotional responses, and most importantly, the principal themes or attitudes, noting especially those that are false or negative.
2. The therapist should then make up a story to explain how and why any evident false themes developed, and how they negatively changed the client's life.
3. Halfway through the story, the therapist should switch the themes towards a more rational, useful perception. Attach this new perception to a value higher in the client's hierarchy. Identify the positive changes that occur to the main characters in the story because of the new perception. (McMullin, 2000, p. 418)

McMullin suggests that for certain clients, e.g. victims of post traumatic stress disorder (PTSD), a few short stories are not sufficient to overcome the thought that the antecedents are just too powerful to be coped with, therefore changing and enhancing belief work is also needed. He also suggests recommending books that illustrate people overcoming adversity by changing or enhancing their beliefs.

The following story 'The noise' can be used to illustrate that how people behave in a situation is influenced by their thinking. It's not what happens to you that is significant but how you think about what happens to you:

THE NOISE

Early one morning, after a late night of playing cards, a group of friends are woken up by a strange rustling sound downstairs. The first man jumps up, believing the noise to be made by a burglar and after looking around for a weapon, picks up a baseball bat, and cries 'I'll give them something to think about!'. The second man, whose house it is, thinks that his wife, who objects to his gambling, has returned early from an overseas trip and panics because he knows the telltale cards and empty beer cans are still lying about downstairs. The third man thinks that the strange noise is coming from the heater he has just fitted for his friend whose house it is, and sighs deeply, mumbling 'I can't do anything right.' The fourth man thinks it is the paperboy and calmly goes downstairs to find him still struggling to put the large Sunday papers through the letter box.

In this story, the thoughts and beliefs of each person hearing the noise bring varied responses. The thinking of the first three individuals leads to anger, anxiety and depression respectively, while the fourth man interprets the sound more accurately, which brings a calm and accurate response or behaviour.

At this point, let us return to some of the territory we mentioned earlier, concerning the new perspectives that have been brought to bear on the territory of attitudes, especially where they emphasise flexibility and diversity. One of the significant features of European social psychology over the last 20 years has been a turn to language, discourse and communication. To sum up the thrust of this movement, it tends towards the belief that human beings are extremely flexible in the way that they are able to think and talk about phenomena in the world around them. For almost every attitude based on a generalisation – 'I don't normally like white bread' – there are particularisations and exceptions – 'but I like this because it's better as it's still hot and comes from my local baker'. This particularisation and context dependence sometimes extends to strong affective and visceral responses too. A friend of one of the authors who trained as an operating theatre assistant happily encountered a good deal of blood and guts as part of her everyday work, yet was still extremely squeamish about everyday domestic injuries such as cut fingers and grazes, even though she felt this was irrational herself. This apparent inconsistency has sometimes been referred to as the 'dilemmatic' aspect of attitudes. The approach to social psychology we are talking about then emphasises flexibility and the necessity of examining language for clues as to how people create meaning in situ (Potter & Wetherell, 1987; Edwards & Potter, 1992; Edwards, 1997).

Attitudes, and the associated activities of categorisation and stereotyping, are viewed as discursive practices – that is they are executed within language – which are flexibly articulated within particular social contexts to do certain things, such as to blame, accuse, excuse, persuade, justify and generally construct a coherent account of oneself. In the discursive approach, holding an attitude, assigning an object to a category or making use of a stereotype is something we do in talk in order to accomplish social actions. As Billig (1989) contends, holding attitudes enables us to construct arguments. Such an approach recommends the fine-grained analysis of what is actually said in everyday talk and interaction. This variability in everyday talk is common and easy to see in transcripts, but hidden by the kinds of statistical approaches used by cognitive social psychologists, which are based on averaging data together. Given the existence of this kind of variation in people's talk, attitudes do not appear to exist as stable and consistent entities, and it is little wonder that they are often only weakly related to behaviour. Potter and Wetherell (1987) argue that instead of treating what people say as a manifestation of some kind of internal state or attitude, we should look at what people are doing with their talk and how it functions in everyday interaction or in therapy.

A common observation in therapy is that clients seem to be struggling against attitudes, ideas, intrusive thoughts and distressing symptoms, rather in the manner of the dilemmatic feature of attitudes we mentioned earlier. Sometimes, the harder the clients struggle the more compelling the ideas are. This can be illustrated fairly simply: for instance, try not to think of a blue dog wearing black spectacles and one automatically pops into mind. A client may want to be at peace with him or herself, but at the same time unwanted thoughts are all the more intrusive.

This kind of tendency is illustrated allegorically by Dwivedi (1997):

Milarepa

Milarepa was a famous monk. A gentleman who felt very agitated came to see Milarepa and said that there was always some kind of chattering in his mind and he could not feel restful or peaceful at all. He asked Milarepa for a way of stopping this chattering of the mind. Milarepa said go home and to stop thinking of monkeys. The gentleman said that not thinking of monkeys was not a problem for him, because he never thought of monkeys and they never crossed his mind. Milarepa was delighted to hear this and declared that in that case the practice of 'not thinking about monkeys' should then come very easily to him and that he should go home and continue to practise. The gentleman began to do what he was told, only to realise that the more he tried not to think of monkeys, the more he ended up thinking of monkeys.

This technique, encapsulated in an Indian folktale, has been elaborated in Western psychotherapy too. Sometimes it is referred to as 'paradoxical intention', a phrase coined by Viktor Frankl (1975). This may take the form of positively inviting the thoughts and wishes we seek to avoid. People with panic attacks may be encouraged to positively invite their hearts to beat wildly and gasp for breath. Sometimes it might take the form of 'symptom prescription'. For example, McMullin (2000) describes a technique he calls 'forced catastrophes'. Here, an obsessive client might be asked to spend a specified period checking locks, arranging their possessions or cleaning. A worrisome client might be invited to spend at least 10 minutes an hour doing nothing but worrying. Someone troubled by intrusive thoughts or flashbacks might be encouraged to set aside a specified period of time each day to have these. A compulsive hand-washer might be encouraged to increase the time spent in ablution. The idea is that sooner or later the worry will become boring, the rituals will become absurd or impossible to complete and – perhaps most importantly of all – the technique will introduce some much needed humour into the situation. Thus, it is the attention or indulgence we give to the triggering of imaginary objects that keeps fuelling the psycho-physiological changes characteristic of anxiety. Lazarus (1974) calls this the 'blow up method', where the undesired behaviour or experience is blown up so that it seems ridiculous. For example, he describes a young man who was concerned about his sweaty palms. Lazarus encouraged this client to avoid wiping his hands, to try to spray other people with this excess of sweat and even go outside and wash the cars with his endless flood of sweat. The fantasy therefore becomes absurd and humorous, thus helping to defuse the anxiety associated with the phenomenon. This is also an example of the phenomenon we identified earlier – that of particularisation, identified by the discursive psychological tradition. That is, one way of thinking about the phenomenon we have just described is to see it as an example of this tendency to make particularised exceptions to general attitudes. It's worrying except when it's funny. By helping clients to focus on these exceptions therapists can help them defuse the menacing power of their anxieties.

In the same way that anxiety can be defused, it is also possible to tackle anger. We will say more about this in the discussion of emotions, but for the time being it is worth noting that anger is susceptible to these kinds of interventions. For example, a client angry at the frustrations and difficulties, which they believe others are heaping upon them can be encouraged to explore the following fantasy: imagine yourself as a supreme ruler, a god or goddess who owns the streets and the shops and the office space and to whom everyone defers so that you can have your own way. The more detail the client is encouraged to use in imagining this situation, the more likely it is to seem absurd and can be used as a way of defusing the seriousness of the situation. Therefore, managing anger involves not only developing awareness of the psycho-physiological changes on the one hand, and also of developing techniques to encourage acceptance and more effective ways of dealing with these circumstances and changes. This process is enhanced if we approach the feelings of anger and the accompanying psycho-physiological changes without fighting them, instead easing into them and relaxing into them. With practice it is possible to learn to transmute the emotion into a constructive process, like turning coal into a diamond. It is a longstanding belief among many scholars of emotion that the person's cognitive appraisal plays an important part in the experience of emotion. This stretches from Schacter and Singer's famous experiment over 40 years ago (Schacter & Singer, 1962) to Rom Harre's (1996) more recent contention that emotions represent a kind of value judgement. Dwivedi's conclusion is much the same: cognitive components play a significant role in the mechanisms involved in the emotional system. Perceptions, cognitive appraisals, values and beliefs greatly influence emotions such as anger and are, in turn, shaped by these emotional experiences. Such intricate relationships are further augmented by the fact that our minds often mix the real with the unreal and have a tendency to take things personally.

There are various kinds of problem attitudes that a therapist will observe in their work with clients, and it may be helpful to find stories to illustrate alternative ways of thinking. For example, take the attitude that exposing inadequacies will result in loss of face or humiliation, illustrated by the following story:

CLUELESS

Joseph was a young academic who was hoping to write a book with his colleague, Tony. They had a meeting with a commissioning editor. Joseph was very anxious at the meeting, and grew concerned that the editor, who was very formal in his manner, would find fault with his answers and declare that he was not up to the serious business of writing a book. In contrast, Tony was a picture of calmness. At one point in the meeting the editor turned to Joseph and asked him a very complicated question. Frightened that the editor would not commission the book unless he gave a meaningful answer, Joseph pretended to understand the question but soon dried up when giving his answer. The editor turned to Tony and asked the same question. Grateful that the spotlight had now fallen on his colleague, Joseph watched him fold his arms, pinch his chin and sink into deep thought. After several moments Tony made as if to speak, but then fell quiet again in deliberation of what he had been asked. More time passed and Joseph leaned forward to catch the words of wisdom that he sensed would soon be generated by his colleague. After yet more chin stroking, Tony coughed to announce that he was about to speak and the editor smiled encouragingly. Then he said in a loud, confident voice, 'I haven't got a bloody clue'. To Joseph's surprise the editor laughed openly and then proceeded to discuss the book project in a more animated way and did not appear to think anything less of Tony's subsequent comments.

In this story, Tony's response demonstrates that an individual does not have to have all the answers and that it is acceptable to admit to limitations in knowledge. Sometimes such admissions can enhance human relationships.

Another attitude that commonly restricts a client's behaviour is that if they let out their emotions people might dislike them. Here, the therapist will try to encourage the view that expressing our emotions is healthy because they enable us to have closer relationships with other people and feel better in ourselves. We might bridge this change in attitude in the following story:

GIVING IT BIG

Joanne always kept her feelings bottled up, believing that nobody wants to hear other people's troubles. Her thinking on this had been heavily influenced by the behaviour of her mother who was always outspoken in her opinions. Sometimes, this show of emotion in public left Joanne feeling acutely embarrassed. After work, Joanne and the other secretaries would meet up in the local pub. She liked to keep the conversation light and although she listened closely to what her colleagues had to say, always gave a balanced, unemotional response. On most occasions, she would limit her drinking, or leave early when the atmosphere got lively or, as sometimes happened, arguments broke out. One day she overheard work colleagues talking about her and was shocked to find out that they found her aloof, lacking in warmth and too perfect for words. Joanne slipped back to her desk and tried to get on with her work, although she was upset. After work, as usual, she joined her colleagues in the pub. This time, when her opinion was sought out of habitual politeness, she gave it no holds barred. She gave her opinions 'big' with all the trimmings. She said how she felt about work and fumed about a range of topics from politics and religion to sport and relationships with men. The eyes of her colleagues turned into saucers as she let it all out in an exaggerated, loud voice. 'They want emotion,' she decided, 'I've got plenty put aside!'. Later that night, Joanne, noticed that her colleagues made a fuss of her on leaving, even throwing their arms over her shoulder affectionately. That had never happened before. Although she was never that loud ever again, she had learnt that to express emotions is OK and people don't necessarily dislike you for it. Now she appreciates her own emotions and feels truer to herself.

There will be many clients who have an exaggerated sense of perfectionism. This attitude, although having some advantages, can be unhelpful, as indicated in the following story:

THE PERFECT PICTURE

Molly was a professional painter whose work had been exhibited at small galleries. She was so careful about her work that she often discarded canvases that didn't live up to her expectations. These perfectionistic tendencies had clearly helped in the past to produce some very fine work that had even brought awards, but there were, however, certain downsides. Her desire to produce a great painting got her so anxious that it interfered with her actual painting. She spent so much time and energy on trying to achieve a masterpiece that she neglected the needs of her family who were getting increasingly irritated and frustrated with her. She was hypercritical of her art to the point of not seeing what was good about her work, and getting satisfaction and pleasure from it. She could always find something that was not perfect in her pictures, and then became self-critical and upset. This critical outlook was also turned on the work of fellow artists and over the years she lost a number of friendships on account of her overly harsh judgements. Outside of her painting, her life and activities became quite narrow and unsatisfying. She was limited in her technique and style of painting because she was unwilling to risk mistakes by experimenting with her work, which led to her feeling bored and restless in turn as she was being offered no new challenges. Also, her output was so small that she struggled to make ends meet financially.

A client may have rigid, inflexible ideas on how to do things and suffers when their plan goes 'wrong'. Yet a more spontaneous or organic response might bring greater flexibility and the joy of surprise. The following story demonstrates this shift:

THE PARTY

Sylvia was planning a surprise garden party for her husband Geoff's 50th birthday. The couple had a wonderful large garden at the rear of their tiny cottage. She began preparing for the party two months before the date, making numerous lists of what to buy, whom to invite and so on. She noted in fine detail all the tasks that needed to be done and what times they had to be carried out. It was like a military operation. As the day approached she checked the five-day weather forecast and was pleased to see it would be a dry, if cloudy day. She continued to follow her plan to the letter, ensuring that her husband was invited out to play golf with a close friend while the final preparations were made for the celebration.

With her husband out playing golf on the day of the party, Sylvia and family and friends who came to help began to set up the tables on the lawn and bring out the carefully prepared trays of food. But soon it began to rain heavily. They quickly packed up the tables and took them and the food back into the small cottage. Sylvia was terribly distressed that her plan had been foiled by the weather after all, and sat down and cried. She was angry that despite her fine plan the garden party would have to be cancelled and they would be left to try to entertain all the guests in the cramped rooms of the cottage.

When Maria, a close friend who arrived early to help out, saw Sylvia's plight, she had an idea and checked out the availability of the local church hall, only a short drive from the cottage. She was told that it could be made available for a small fee but they would have to wait until the band using it for rehearsals had finished their session. Maria, Sylvia and other helpers loaded the carefully prepared food, decorations and drinks into cars and went down to the hall. When they went inside a jazz band were still playing. They were very good but Sylvia wanted them to hurry up and pack up their stuff so that she could get everything ready for the party. But when the band finished the number, Maria went up and spoke to them. She seemed to spend a long time chatting and Sylvia grew frustrated. Just when she was about to say something, Maria returned with a beaming smile on her face.

'Wasn't Geoff in a jazz band once?'

'Yes,' answered Sylvia curtly, checking her watch.

'Well the guys up there said they would be happy to play at the party. They wouldn't charge and it would brush up their performance.'

'Well, I hadn't planned having any music,' she said automatically, and then realising just how wonderful it would be to have their very own jazz band, held her hands to her face, tears in her eyes. 'Geoff would love that!'

And Geoff did love that. In fact, he even joined the band for one of his favourite pieces, taking over the drums. Sylvia was delighted to see her husband so happy and vowed never to make rigid plans in future. After the party, Geoff kept in touch with the band members and when their drummer moved on, he took over.

The story illustrates how rigid plans can lay people open to a great deal of frustration and distress when unpredictable things happen. Also, by keeping to such a plan, other opportunities can be missed. The spontaneous approach of Maria provided Sylvia with a more memorable party in the end and even widened Geoff's social network.

Similarly, just as a client may avoid the possibility of things not going to plan, others may find it difficult to deal with conflict and choose to ignore it until it 'goes away'. While the client might feel immediate relief by taking this option, a better solution would be to face and resolve such conflicts as they emerge. For example, in the following story, John 'buries his head in the sand':

THE OSTRICH

John lost his job but was frightened to tell his partner who earned a high salary. He continued his lifestyle as if nothing had happened and soon built up a great amount of debt. He pretended to go out to work every morning and went out in the evenings for meals or drinks. The strain on John increased as the weeks passed and he was still unable to find another job and begin to address his growing debts. But worse still, John found himself having to lie more and more about his situation. His partner would often ask about his day at work and he would make up all kinds of stories. In the mornings he would race down to collect the post just in case his partner saw any of the increasing numbers of unpaid bills and credit card statements. Soon he avoided going home at all so as not to be quizzed about work and spin more lies. With avoiding his partner so much, their relationship began to deteriorate. Even though he knew that his partner could easily cover the debts and would understand his predicament and the need to lie, he just couldn't bring himself to say anything.

Then one day he was passing time in the local library when he caught sight of a wall mural made by visiting schoolchildren. It was the image of an ostrich, standing tall and proud, with no sand in sight. John knew from that moment on that although his partner would be cross and angry if he told the truth of what was happening, and how he had lied to cover up, there would at least be the chance of a fresh start.

In this story, we see that avoiding problem situations or events will only make things worse in the long run. Avoidance can compound problems as the real issues become harder and harder to address in an appropriate way. In other words, 'sticking one's head in the sand' or becoming an 'ostrich' is potentially calamitous.

In a situation where a client may feel helpless and unhappy that her family are not meeting her needs, even when she tells them exactly what these are, an alternative approach would be to look at having those needs met elsewhere. The following story 'The tigress and the piglets' attempts to illustrate this:

THE TIGRESS AND THE PIGLETS

In the farm section of a zoo, a sow gave birth to eight piglets but soon afterwards lost interest in them. In fact, the sow refused to suckle them and even grew aggressive, killing one of them. The remaining piglets continued to approach their mother but still she would have nothing to do with them. The zookeeper saw all this and had to make a quick decision so as to preserve the lives of the litter. He moved the piglets to a separate pen before hitting on an idea of what to do. At the far end of the zoo was a tigress that had recently lost both her cubs, and the zookeeper thought it might be worth the risk of introducing the piglets to her. He removed them from their pen and took them to the tiger enclosure. Amazingly, the tigress immediately took to the little creatures, suckled and played with them. The piglets thrived in the company of the tigress and people came from all over to witness the strange event.

In this story, we are shown that clients' needs do not have to be met by any particular individual, such as their parents, or family members, but can be met by others. Indeed, as in the story, help and support may come from unexpected quarters.

An example from Gergen et al. (1996, p. 115) provides an illustration of how getting an acceptable formulation of the situation can set the stage for effective therapeutic change. The authors describe a group exercise in family therapy where a couple's problems were discussed by reflecting teams. The example reads as follows:

I remember one incident involving a stormy couple who couldn't stay together and couldn't stay apart. One audience group had commented that the couple seemed to have an addiction to crisis. Another group, referring to a local spot which was known as the Bungee Capital of North America, likened their relationship to a pair of married bungee jumpers. The couple objected to the first idea, but warmly accepted the second. Operations like this replace the usual expert model for diagnosis with a less pejorative one.

That is, framing the situation with an appropriate metaphor can render the situation intelligible and circumvent the sometimes intimidating formulations, which expert mental heath discourse sometimes superimposes.

Martin Barker develops a way of making sense of the relationship between readers and stories, which has some resonance with what we are describing here. Barker proposes that a story – especially one which appeals to us – has an agenda that is based on 'living out an unwritten contract with its readers' (1989, p. 165). The 'contract' is premised on active engagement of the reader or listener with the story – the magazine invites a reader to collaborate by reading in particular ways (p. 261): 'The "contract" involves an agreement that a text will talk to us in ways we recognize. It will enter into a dialogue with us. And that dialogue, with its dependable elements and form, will relate to some aspects of our lives in our society.' Barker points out that the contractual understanding between the stories and their implied readers are reliant on their social context. The act of reading can be seen as a process capable of creating feelings of mutual recognition and familiarity between the reader and the features of the story and the storyteller. Barker's reading of popular comics emphasises the interactive engagement of the reader with the storyteller, where both parties are involved in a conversation premised on shared social experiences and expecta-tions (Kehily, 1999).

Finally, in trying to make sense of the relationship between storytelling, attitudes and cognitive behavioural therapies, let us end with a dilemma of our own about what these concepts might mean and how the literary traditions of storytelling might be reconciled with the avowedly scientific spirit of cognitive behavioural therapy. How, exactly, are stories, attitudes and mood related? Aaron Beck's (1967) original formulation of depression and anxiety proposed that some people were prone to holding negative self beliefs and attitudes – 'If I am not highly successful then I am a loser' – and that these latent depressive attitudes become reactivated when an individual is exposed to stress. The sense that one is a loser may remain dormant until one is faced with some sort of setback in an achievement area, whereupon it contributes once more to the downward spiral of depression (Beck & Butler, 1997). Equally, there is some evidence from studies of the thinking of depressed and non-depressed individuals that when the cluster of 'depressogenic' attitudes resolves, then so too does the depression (Cottraux, 1997). People who have recovered from depression have attitudes very similar to those who have never been depressed (Persons & Miranda, 1992; Wenzlaff et al., 2002). Cognitive therapies are also believed to be more effective in preventing relapses than drug therapy for depression (Cottrauz, 1997; Burns & Spangler, 2001).

Cognitive behavioural therapies, then, have their roots firmly in an enlighten-ment paradigm of science, technology and rationality. Indeed, it is common for accounts of cognitive therapy to liken the therapist and client to scientists, and their attitude to therapy is described as one of collaborative empiricism as they explore the client's subjective world and propose hypotheses to be tested. It is almost as if they recreate in miniature the world of scientific inquiry itself. The role of metaphor, story and imagination in this therapeutic world might seem at first difficult to reconcile with the self consciously scientific spirit of therapeutic enquiry. The position of stories and metaphors in this process, however, is extremely important. As Gentner and Jeziorski (1993, pp. 447–8) argue:

Analogy and metaphor are central to scientific thought. They figure in discovery, as in Rutherford's analogy of the solar system for the atom or Faraday's use of lines of magnetized iron filings to reason about electric fields. They are also used in teaching: novices are told to think of electricity as analogous to water flowing through pipes or of a chemical process as analogous to a ball rolling down a hill. Yet for all its usefulness, analogical thinking is never formally taught to us. We seem to think of it as a natural human skill, and of its use in science as a straightforward extension of its use in commonsense reasoning. For example, William James believed that "men, taken historically, reason by analogy long before they have learned to reason by abstract characters". All this points to an appealing intuition: that a faculty for analogical reasoning is an innate part of human cognition.

Storytelling, then, is older and more modern – indeed postmodern – than the earnest search after attitude change formulas and cognitive restructuring techniques that characterised the latter half of the twentieth century. Although storytelling and therapy emerge from different traditions, there are some highly suggestive points of contact. Storytelling techniques, literary and cultural scholarship, and the epistemological shifts involved in the transition to postmodernist and discursive psychologies are different again, yet there are some useful points of intersection. The mid-twentieth century dreams of Beck and Ellis that clusters of dysfunctional attitudes and beliefs might be optimally re-engineered in the name of happiness can be more fully brought to fruition through the incorporation of story, metaphor and literary scholarship.

REFERENCES

Ajzen, I. (1982) On behaving in accordance with one's attitudes. In M. P. Zanna, E. T. Higgins & C. P. Herman (Eds.). *Consistency in social behaviour: The Ontario symposium*. Hillsdale, NJ: Erlbaum.

Barker, M. (1989) *Comics: ideology, power and the critics*. Manchester: Manchester University Press.

Beck, A.T. (1967) *Depression: Clinical, experimental and theoretical aspects*. New York: Harper & Row.

Beck, A.T. (1991) Cognitive therapy: A thirty year retrospective. *American Psychologist*, **46**(4), 368–75.

Beck, J. S. & Butler, A. C. (1997) Cognitive vulnerability to depression. *World Psychiatric Association Bulletin on Depression*, **4**(14), 3–4.

Beutler, L. E., Rocco, F., Molerio, C. M. & Talebi, H. (2001) Resistance, *Psychotherapy: Theory, Research, Practice, Training*, **38**(4), 431–6.

Billig, M. (1989) The argumentative nature of holding strong views: A case study. *European Journal of Social Psychology*, **19**, 203–23.

Burns, D. D. (1999) *Feeling good: The new mood therapy.* New York: Avon.

Burns, D. D & Spangler, D. L. (2001) Do changes in dysfunctional attitudes mediate changes in depression and anxiety in cognitive behavioural therapy? *Behaviour Therapy*, **32**(2), 337–69.

Cottraux, J. (1997) Cognitive therapy for depression. *World Psychiatric Association Bulletin on Depression*, **4**(14), 7–9.

Eagle, M. (1999) Why don't people change? A psychoanalytic perspective. *Journal of Psychotherapy Integration*, **9**(1), 3–32.

Diamond, J. (1999) *C: Because cowards get cancer too...* London: Vermilion.

Dwivedi, K. N. (Ed.)(1997) *The therapeutic use of stories.* London: Routledge.

Edwards, D. (1997) *Discourse and cognition.* London: Sage.

Edwards, D. & Potter, J. (1992) *Discursive psychology.* London: Sage.

Fish, S. (1980) *Is there a text in this class? The authority of interpretive communities.* Cambridge, Mass.: Harvard University Press.

Frank, A. (1995) *The wounded storyteller: Body, illness and ethics.* Chicago, Ill.: University of Chicago Press.

Frank, A. (1997) Narrative witness to bodies: A response to Alan Radley. *Body and Society*, **3**(3), 103–9.

Frank, A. (1998) Stories of illness as care of the self: A Foucaldian dialogue. *Health*, **2**(3), 329–48.

Frankl, V. E. (1975). Paradoxical intention and a reflection. *Psychotherapy*, **12**, 226–40.

Furlong, M. & Oei, T. P. S. (2002) Changes to automatic thoughts and dysfunctional attitudes in group CBT for depression. *Behavioural and Cognitive Psychotherapy*, **30**(3), 351–60.

Gadamer, H. G. (1960) *Truth and method.* New York: Seabury.

Gentner, D. & Jeziorski, M. (1993) The shift from metaphor to analogy in Western science. In A. Ortony (Ed.). *Metaphor and thought* (2nd edn). Cambridge: Cambridge University Press.

Gergen, K. J. (1994) *Toward transformation in social knowledge.* London: Sage Publications.

Gergen, K. (1997) Social psychology as social construction: The emerging vision. In C. McGarty & S. A. Haslam (Eds.). *The message of social psychology: Perspectives on mind in society.* Oxford: Blackwell.

Gergen, K. J., Hoffman, L. & Anderson, H. (1996) Is diagnosis a disaster? A constructionist trialogue. In F. W. Kaslow (Ed.). *Handbook of relational diagnosis and dysfunctional family patterns.* New York: Wiley.

Gersie, A. (1997) *Reflections on therapeutic storymaking: The use of stories in groups.* London: Jessica Kingsley Publishers.

Gramling, L. F. & McCain, N. L. (1997) Grey glasses: Sadness in young women. *Journal of Advanced Nursing*, **26**, 312–19.

Harre, R. (1986) *The social construction of emotions.* Oxford: Blackwell.

Hauck, P. A. (2001) When reason is not enough. *Journal of Rational Emotive and Cognitive Behaviour Therapy*, **19**(4), 245–57.

Hovland, C., Janis, I. & Kelley, E. C. (1953) *Communication and persuasion: Psychological studies of attitude change.* New Haven, Conn.: Yale University Press.

Jenkins, W. W. (2001) Resistance. In H. G. Kadso & C. E. Schaefer (Eds.). *A hundred and one more favourite play therapy techniques.* Northvale, NJ: Jason Aronson.

Jowett, G. S. & O'Donnell, V. (1992) *Propaganda and persuasion.* London: Sage.

Karp, D. A. (1992) Illness ambiguity and the search for meaning. *Journal of Contemporary Ethnography*, **21**, 139–70.

Karp, D. A. (1993) Taking anti-depressant medications: Resistance, trial commitment, conversion, disenchantment. *Qualitative Sociology*, **16**(4), 337–59.

Kehily, M. J. (1999) More sugar? Teenage magazines, gender displays and sexual learning. *European Journal of Cultural Studies*, **2**(1), 65–89.

Kinney, A. (2000) The intellectual insight problem: Implications for assessment and rational emotive behaviour therapy. *Journal of Contemporary Psychotherapy*, **30**(3), 261–72.

Krafft-Ebing, R. Von (1886/1975) *Psychopathia sexualis*. New York: Putnam.

Lankton, C. H. & Lankton, S. R. (1989) *Tales of enchantment: Goal oriented metaphors for adults and children in therapy*. New York: Brunner/Mazel.

Lankton, S. R., Lankton, C. H. & Erickson, M. (1986) *Enchantment and intervention in family therapy: Training in Ericksonian approaches*. New York: Brunner/Mazel.

Lazarus, A. (1974). *Clinical behavior therapy*. New York: Brunner/Mazel.

Lee, E & Leets, L. (2002) Persuasive storytelling by hate groups online: Examining the effects on adolescents. *American Behavioral Scientist*, **45**(6), 927–57.

Leedy, J. (1985) Principles of poetry therapy. In J. Leedy (Ed.). *Poetry as healer: Mending the troubled mind*. New York: Vanguard Press.

Leyden-Rubenstein, L. (2001) Peace on earth begins with inner peace. *Annals of the American Psychotherapy Association*, **4**(6), 24.

Lindlof, T. (1988) Media audiences as interpretive communities. *Communication Yearbook*, **11**, 81–107.

Maoz, I. & Bar-On, D. (2002) *From working through the holocaust to current ethnic conflicts: Evaluating the current TRT group workshop in Hamburg*, Group, **26**(1), 29–48.

McGuire, W. J. (1985) Attitudes and attitude change. In G. Lindzey & E. Aronson (Eds.). *The handbook of social psychology* (3rd edn), vol. 2. New York: Random House.

McMullin. R. E. (2000) *Handbook of cognitive therapy techniques*. New York: W. W. Norton.

Naisbitt, J. (1982) *Megatrends*. New York: Warner.

Persons, K. B. & Miranda, J. (1992) Cognitive theories of vulnerability to depression: Reconciling negative evidence. *Cognitive Therapy and Research*, **16**, 485–502.

Potter, J. & Wetherell, M. (1987) *Discourse and social psychology: Beyond attitudes and behaviour*. London and Beverly Hills, Calif: Sage.

Priester, J., Wegener, D., Petty, R. & Fabrigar, L (1999) Examining the psychological process underlying the sleeper effect: The elaboration likelihood model explanation, *Media-Psychology*, **1**(1), 27–48.

Radway, J. (1984) *Reading the romance*. Chapel Hill: University of North Carolina Press.

Rasmussen, P. R. (2002) Resistance: The fear behind it and tactics for reducing it. *Journal of Individual Psychology*, **58**(2), 148–59.

Reed, M. A. (1999) Contributions of Shakespeare's Paulina to the contempary practice of poetry therapy. *The Arts in Psychotherapy*, **26**(2), 103–10.

Schacter, S. & Singer, J. E. (1962) Cognitive, social and physiological determinants of emotional state. *Psychological Review*, **69**, 379–99.

Shah, I. (1979) *World tales*. Harmondsworth: Penguin Books.

Strong, T. (2002) Dialogue in therapy's 'borderzone'. *Journal of Constructivist Psychology*, **15**(4), 245–62.

Walkerdine, V., Lucey, H. & Melody, J. (2001) *Growing up girl: Psychosocial explorations of gender and class*. Basingstoke: Palgrave.

Weintraub, M., Segal, R. M. & Beck, A. T. (1974) An investigation of cognition and affect in the depressive experience of normal men. *Journal of Consulting and Clinical Psychology*, **42**, 911.

Weissman, A. & Beck, A. T. (1978) Development and validation of the dysfunctional attitude scale. Paper presented at the Annual Meeting of the Association for the Advancement of Behaviour Therapy, Chicago, Ill.

Weissman, A. & Beck, A. T. (1979) The dysfunctional attitude scale: A validation study. *Dissertation Abstracts International*, **40**, 1389.

Wenzlaff, R. M., Rude, S. S. & West, L. M. (2002) Cognitive vulnerability to depression: The role of thought suppression and attitude certainty. *Cognition and Emotion*, **16**(4), 533–48.

3 EMOTIONS

This chapter examines how therapists can use stories as another method to assist with changing emotions. Achieving a shift in the client's emotions is far from straightforward. Moreover, no matter how well trained the therapist is, there will inevitably be times when the therapist has to confront particularly difficult situations or difficult clients, and will have to come to terms with their own emotions. It is our contention that stories, anecdotes and metaphors can help with all of these complex and difficult situations. By the time they are old enough to undertake therapy, the majority of people will have become familiar with a wide range of emotions such as fear, anger, sadness, happiness and surprise. Emotions are often considered key to therapeutic change, so it is only fitting that we have a chapter that focuses on how stories can be used to change affect or emotion.

The idea of changing emotions through talking to people and having them talk to the therapist might seem a little strange. Although we emphasise how cognitions/attitudes affect the way we feel, within psychology there is an important strand of thinking, which tells us that emotions are relatively independent of cognition. The transmission of sensory energy to emotional reactions is held to be independent of consciousness and involves no mediation or transformation of information (Izard & Buechler, 1980, p. 180; Zajonc, 1980, pp. 84, 154). Izard (1984, p. 24) explicitly states that 'emotion has no cognitive component. I maintain that the emotion process is bounded by the feeling that derives directly from the activity of the neurochemical substrates.' Izard and Buechler (1980, p. 173) propose that emotions are related to naturally elicited facial expressions, which are determined by intrinsic processes in the somatic nervous system. In Izard and Buechler's model, sensory feedback from the face produces autonomic arousal and emotional experience. This kind of argument has been called the 'naturalistic position'. It is often associated with the notion that emotions derive from so-called primitive brain structures and are somehow natural and inevitable (Zajonc, 1980; 1984). As Zajonc himself puts it: 'preferences need no inferences'. Emotions are a kind of 'snappy crocodile' left over from our evolutionary past.

Emotions, then, could well turn out to be a tough nut to crack from the point of view of the storytelling therapist. Scientific-sounding accounts like these imply that it is pretty hopeless to say a few words and expect the situation to improve. Added to this, clients often feel overwhelmed by sadness, grief or anger, as if it were outside their conscious control. As an eight-year-old child, known to one of the authors, said when questioned about the way he so often assaulted his brother: 'My brain gets angry and I can't help it'.

Fortunately this is not the whole story as far as theories of emotion are concerned. There are a number of other scholars, such as Rom Harre (for example, Harre & Gillett, 1994) and Wendy Hollway (for example, 1984; 1989), who have drawn attention to the way emotions are deeply embedded in our social lives as human beings and are intimately connected with the kinds of stories we tell. This is fortunate for us as therapists because it highlights the way that stories and emotions go hand in hand. The snappy crocodile of the 'naturalistic' theorists can sometimes be persuaded to be a more sociable creature. Harre, for example, sees emotions as being embedded in the narratives and symbolic displays of everyday life. According to this view one should ask what judgements emotions express and what social acts they are used to perform. Hollway believed that emotions could be understood to work within a 'positioning triad' of three key elements in an emotional episode:

1. The storyline evolving in an episode.
2. The relative positions of the speakers with respect to the local conventions of displaying emotions.
3. The social acts the speakers are trying to perform.

If we take an example like grief at a funeral there are differing conventions in different countries. In the UK it is common for people to have a serious demeanour but florid displays of crying are unusual. On the other hand, in Eastern Mediterranean countries displays of grief can be very flamboyant. Indeed, sometimes there might be professional mourners who put on a good show of lamenting for the other guests.

According to Theodore Sarbin (1987), it is important to see emotions as meaningful displays that are performed according to social conventions. Like language, emotional displays have an 'illocutionary force' – they have an executive function. That is, often emotions are telling other people to do something. There are, says Sarbin, 'dramatistic conventions' to the display of emotion. If we take the example of anger, nowadays it generally refers to an internal state of consciousness, but a few hundred years ago anger was a kind of social action (Stearns & Stearns, 1986). If we recall the 'angry and jealous God' of the King James English translation of the Bible this exemplifies the way that anger was about making other people do one's bidding. In secular life and politics it was intimately connected with disposing of one's rivals and succeeding in conflict. These conventions of display are apparent with other feelings too. When one of us was in hospital a few years ago, it was intriguing to contrast the stiff upper lip and restrained, occasional groans of the English patients with the behaviour of an elderly Polish gentleman who was brought in one night. He lamented very volubly and at length, in keeping with his mid-European heritage. Agitated nurses could be heard saying things like 'We've got to keep him quiet' to one another. It was almost as if his cries offended against the orderliness of the hospital. This incident underscores another key feature of emotions – they often offend against order.

Harre and Gillett (1994) argue that emotions are 'intentional' acts - actions done for a purpose. There are 'right' and 'wrong' ways to perform the emotional display in different contexts. A student of one of the authors did a project which involved interviewing medical doctors about their experience of stress at home and at work, and discovered that the death of a patient, while it might evoke strong emotions, was dealt with relatively quickly, by comparison with family bereavements, which were typically associated with much longer periods of grieving and readjustment.

According to Harre and Gillett (1994), there are three different kinds of judgements that might go into making up an emotion:

1. Moral judgements – for example, anger that expresses the point of view that another person has performed a transgression of some sort.
2. Aesthetic judgements – for example, 'disgust' seems to be associated with the sense that the object of the feeling would be unpleasant to touch.
3. Prudential judgements – for example, fear is about a judgement that the object of the fear is dangerous.

As James Averill explained, in the relationship between culture, consciousness, and emotions, 'the emotions are viewed here as transitory social roles, or socially constituted syndromes. The social norms that help to constitute these syndromes are represented psychologically as cognitive structures or schemata. These structures – like the grammar of a language – provide the basis for the appraisal of stimuli, the organization of responses, and the monitoring of behaviour' (Averill, 1980, pp. 305–6).

We have all experienced the power of stories to evoke certain emotions, such as fear when listening to a ghost story or watching a horror film. Burns (2001) notes how professional Tibetan storytellers told epic legends of battles and bravery to evoke emotions of courage; while in Nepal, instead of corporal punishment, mothers use frightening stories to control their children; and in the islands of Fiji ancient stories are told to empower certain people with the self control to enable them to perform actions such as fire-walking.

This kind of storytelling also has a social place in the telling of factual events too. In a fascinating account of the use of emotions in newspaper reporting, Michael Barton (in Stearns & Lewis, 1998) provides an analysis of the emotional tenor of American newspaper reporting of human tragedies from the 1850s to the 1950s. Reporting on the human devastation of floods, marine and rail accidents, and state executions – what Barton refers to as 'journalistic gore' – provided a space for the public expression of a wide range of difficult emotions. Documenting a historical shift in the expression of emotion that follows the trajectory which Peter Stearns has tracked from 'Victorian "passion" ... to a modern "cool" style', Barton finds a historical drift 'toward more information than story, more sobriety than empathy, more discretion than gore' (p. 107). For example, he notes the emotional involvement and florid sentimentality of nineteenth-century reporting. A reporter's description of an 1854 railway accident near Baltimore is typical: 'Awful catastrophe. Horrible accident ... The scene was most dreadful.... The rear car passing entirely through the foremost one, and both being filled with passengers, the destruction of life and limb was almost unprecedented. ... Among the dead was Mrs. Roberson, a young and beautiful woman ... In removing the cars Mrs. Roberson's body was literally torn to pieces' (p. 109). As Barton notes, this kind of blatantly emotional reporting was gradually replaced by detailed yet detached body counts, references to previous record accidents and more focus on the fortunate survivors than the unfortunate victims. Our late-twentieth-century exposure to death and destruction via global satellite news provides such 'detached detail' to an extreme degree; here, image and information are separated from their emotional grounding in ways that would have been unimaginable to Americans a century ago.

These historical changes may be interesting but they do not necessarily yield practical insights for therapists and clients. Nevertheless they show how emotions are related to the social context in which they are evoked. If we can use stories to somehow shift the context then we may well be on the way towards changing emotions.

In the 1960s psychologists became interested in what was called the two factor theory of emotion. This involved thinking of emotions as involving a state of physiological arousal and a cognitive label, following Schacter and Singer's (1962) landmark experiment on how people identify their own emotional states. This study suggested that once people became aware that they were physiologically aroused they tried to find possible causes to which this could be attributed. Those who believed it was due to a dose of adrenaline they had been given were less emotional, whereas others who had no such explanation tended to follow the emotional tone of the situation. Thus in some conditions they were paired with a confederate of the experimenter who reacted angrily to an insulting questionnaire they were asked to fill in ('How many extramarital affairs did your mother have? (a) less than 10, (b) between 10 and 20 ...' and so on). Participants here tended to feel angry. On the other hand, those paired with a confederate who acted humorously, tended to become euphoric too. The overall drift of this line of work was that social cues and attributions were crucial in making sense of emotional states. As soon as this idea gained currency, however, people with a psychotherapeutic focus felt there was something lacking in this idea. It did not quite explain why emotions were so difficult to change in therapy, even when the client agreed that they were maladaptive. Thus in the early 1960s Albert Ellis (1963) attempted to explain this difficulty by distinguishing between 'intellectual-insight' and 'emotional-insight'. This distinction is important to the practice of rational-emotive behaviour therapy (REBT). According to Ellis (1963), intellectual-insight implies that the client knows or understands that he or she is disturbed and that his or her behaviour is self defeating. It is 'an acknowledgment that an irrational belief frequently leads to emotional disturbance and dysfunctional behaviour and that a rational belief almost always abets emotional health' (Ellis & Dryden, 1997, p. 42). By contrast, emotional-insight is defined as 'a very strong and frequently held belief that an irrational idea is dysfunctional and that a rational idea is helpful' (Ellis & Dryden, 1997, p. 42). Furthermore, emotional-insight, according to Ellis (1963), is a 'radically different, essentially more forceful, effective, and committed kind of behaviour'. In this case, the person genuinely believes and undertakes change (Ellis, 1963).

Sometimes attempts on the part of therapists to manage people's emotions are actively counterproductive. Not only can people still be troubled by unpleasant and socially undesirable emotions even when they know it is not good for them to do so, but also change attempts themselves can have the opposite effect to what was intended. A student introduced one of the authors to her father who had for many years suffered from an anxiety disorder. Although able to go into work most of the time and participate in family life to a certain extent, he persistently suffered from moments of panic, feelings of uncomfortable tension and irritability. His clinical psychologist had attempted the usual approach of teaching relaxation skills and had given him a number of relaxation tapes. The unfortunate client had become increasingly annoyed at the supposedly soothing American voice and what he described as the 'warbly music'. Apparently, he would diligently sit fuming with his brow furrowed and jaw clenched, trying to use the relaxation tapes as directed, and then shout at his family.

Thus, despite the fact that clients might accept therapeutic wisdom about their emotions, sometimes the feelings themselves are not so easily fooled. This is why stories are so useful. By providing a memorable and clear story that evokes an adaptive response to such emotions, the client may be empowered to pull him or herself from their own 'barbed wire'. That is, like being trapped in wire, brambles or roses, struggling and pulling may be instinctive but relaxing and allowing the barbs to release may be a more productive strategy. Such adaptation may simply involve learning to accept the factuality of various life pressures, normalising the emotions that can result from 'dealing with life' and exploring the possibilities of changing those things that can be changed.

Stories may be used didactically to teach a strategy or alter a perception. A therapeutic group for clients with eating disorders that one of us came across was led by a facilitator who used a great many metaphors of control concerned with eating and appetite. The clients often exercised an iron-willed restraint punctuated by uncontrolled binges. The facilitator used a couple of ideas that merit retelling. One was the grasping of a handful of sand. The tighter you try to hold it the more it squeezes out between your fingers. To 'gain control' of the sand you had to give up a little control by counter-intuitively picking it up gently with an open hand. Likewise a story was told of members of an African culture, who captured chimpanzees by putting tasty morsels of food in hollow containers with small openings. The chimps would put their hands inside to grasp the food but the opening was too small to allow the clenched fist to exit. The unfortunate chimp would stay there grasping the food and trying to pull its hand out until the arrival of the human captors. Again, the idea of the analogy is to encourage people to give up the iron-willed control they exerted over their appetites, as the desire for control had come to control them.

While some stories might be overtly didactic, like the foregoing examples, some might work precisely by not challenging the clients directly but by being allusive. Clients who have experienced a number of damaging life events, such as major losses or even possibly early abusive experiences, may experience hopelessness and a sense that nothing can be done to improve their situation. It is often difficult to tackle this. Indeed, for those recovering from such experiences, supportive interventions from friends and therapists may be particularly difficult to accept. The use of stories might help bring about emotional changes in such situations. In these cases, anecdotes introduce the potential benefits of clients taking small steps to change the way they view their situation. Anecdotes afford short-cuts, which encapsulate these changes and make the formula for change memorable to clients. For instance, one of the authors worked with a client who faced a number of challenges relating to his physical health, marriage and work. He presented clinically with depression and anxiety symptoms and the following story 'Learning a new trick' was given:

LEARNING A NEW TRICK

Barry had a number of difficulties in his life, such as poor health, being unhappy in his marriage, his close friend moving away and having to deal with his son who was forever in trouble at school. To make matters worse, his dull office job intensified a sense of powerlessness and made him feel low. Colleagues did not show any particular interest in him or, when they did, it was only to be critical about his work. As the weeks passed, he struggled to deal with his emotions and felt there was little to look forward to in the future.

One day, on his way to work, he chanced upon a book about magic that someone had either lost or discarded. He decided to read it and was surprised at how easy some of the tricks were. When he had learnt two or three tricks and practised them in private he decided to risk trying them out on his work colleagues. To his surprise they enjoyed the tricks he performed and even encouraged him to repeat them to other colleagues. Heartened by their response he learnt a few more tricks to add to his repertoire. In time, his mini-performances brought him into friendly conversations with those around him. With each new trick he learned, Barry looked forward to trying it out at work during coffee or lunch break. Through his effort the atmosphere at work gradually changed. While the problems with his health and relationships with his wife and son were still there, the better atmosphere at work gave him more energy to try to deal with them when he got home. Reflecting on his circumstances he realised that apart from the good fortune in finding the book, the real magic lay in taking a first, small step to change one aspect of his circumstances. In doing that he had learnt a new and powerful trick.

Therapy then proceeded by asking this client what he thought about the story and whether it might have any personal meaning for him. He was able to see that perhaps focusing on changing one small aspect of life may be helpful. Hitherto his problems taken all together had seemed overwhelming to him. He chose to make more effort in pursuing a more satisfying social life. He was encouraged to look at ways that he could take the initiative with friends rather than simply waiting for their contact. In doing this the difficulty for the client in breaking his established habits to make these changes was not underestimated. Improvements were not immediate for him but gradually over time his mood improved. Stories, then, can enable us to tackle small aspects of the problem rather than large ones, and enable an indirect approach that does not immediately activate defences.

In order to increase the possible effectiveness of this story, when telling it, we might emphasise or embellish the hopelessness of the man's predicament. The therapist can add various other 'intensifiers' such as financial difficulties, as she sees fit, keeping them of similar severity but perhaps subtly different from the client's own life. While using a story like this, it is a good idea to monitor the client's identification with the story by watching for any sign of recognition or emotion, especially if it appears to resonate with the emotion points in the story, as misfortune is heaped on misfortune. If the story works for the client, it can be used to get them to identify with the hopeless situation of the protagonist and how one tiny attempt to make a change in his circumstances resulted in major emotional changes. Emphasise here how choosing to do something differently and, if you like, take a small step to changing one's world, can result in unexpected benefits. Of course, it might not be realistic to convey the impression that everything became rosy for the character in the story. Problems still existed, but the person began to view things differently. This follows the principle that it's not always what happens to you externally, or in the outside world, that is important, but how you respond internally, in the way you think about yourself in the world. This can involve some reflection about the kinds of aspects of a client's life they can change for the better. They might make a person smile, they might gain acceptance or they might alleviate someone's boredom. This might not solve their problems outright but it will go some way towards putting in place the social support network they will be able to make use of in order to tackle things effectively. A good way to finish a session based around this anecdote would be to ask the client for their thoughts and reiterate the fact that maybe they too can take a small step to improve how they feel.

Emotional involvement is widely acknowledged as being important in a good deal of advice given to storytellers, poets and dramatists. The role of stories in enlisting the hearers into particular feelings, from exaggerated hissing at pantomime villains to apprehension and suspense in an adventure story has often been noted, yet we are still unsure of how it works and we have searched in vain for a means of putting it on a sound theoretical basis. One such attempt that stands out is Ien Ang's work on the popular 1980s soap opera *Dallas* (Ang, 1985). This is interesting to us as she was specifically interested in what she called the 'tragic structure of feeling' in the programme. Working from written accounts of the experience of watching the programmes from a number of participants she identified some common themes. They saw the series as realistic yet it depicted wealthy business people in the United States, very different from everyday life for ordinary people in Ang's native Holland. However, the realism they perceived was at the level of emotions – the characters cried, fought and became alcoholic. However, even here there was a perceived discrepancy between the likely behaviour of ordinary people and the exaggerated displays of the soap opera. Yet they still believed it was realistic. Perhaps it was realistic in the sense of fitting in with their understanding of the social conventions of emotional experience and expression.

Thus, in making sense of emotions and fitting them into a story the therapist needs to be rather like an anthropologist, in understanding the strange 'tragic structures of feeling' deployed by clients and also found in the common culture within which therapy takes place. While emotions clearly have physiological aspects, our ability to identify, respond to and make sense of emotions depends on a good deal of implicit social knowledge. James Averill, whom we mentioned earlier, calls emotions *syndromes,* that is, clusters or sets of responses. In his view, we learn how to label, respond to and perform emotions through communication with others. Most emotions have a particular range of *objects* at which we direct the emotion. That is, when we speak of love and anger, these are usually directed at people, rather than, say, tables and chairs. We learn about emotions through social interaction, and rules that are learned throughout life. Averill's view of emotions has a good deal in common with the view of emotion implicit in a good deal of psychotherapy, particularly when therapists speak of the desirability of altering people's appraisals or cognitive restructuring so as to reduce negative feelings. According to Averill, there are four kinds of rules that may determine how we respond to our feelings and emotions:

1. Rules of appraisal, which help us identify the type, direction and positive or negative nature of an emotion and help us link social cues to internal feelings and states.
2. Rules of behaviour, which guide our choice of response to an emotion private or public, calm or aggressive. For example, where we feel that something is amiss but worry over whether it's appropriate to 'say something'.
3. Rules of prognosis, which help us know the cause, progress and course of an emotion. That is, social commonplaces like 'You'll feel better after a good cry' might count as 'rules of prognosis'.
4. Rules of attribution, which determine how we rationalise or justify an emotion. That is, we might attribute a sense of negative arousal feelings to the people around us even if it is not their fault.

It is often the case that feelings, emotions and sentiments bring people into contact with a therapist. People may have the most unlikely or bizarre experiences and carry on with their lives as usual, provided they are not distressed by these events. It is the emotional tone of experiences that turn them from everyday occurrences into clinically significant entities. There are many examples of stories that have helped people with such difficulties. For instance, Burns (2001) describes the story of Captain Scott's expedition to the Antarctic being an inspiration to troops in World War 1. Scott's widow was known to have received many letters assuring her that her husband's story had helped them to manage the adversities of trench life and battle. Just as Scott and his team battled with hand-drawn sleds against severe weather conditions, then the soldiers could feel able to persevere with their situation.

This use of description to evoke emotions depends partly on the richness of the description and partly on the cultural background of the audience. A description of a hot bacon sandwich might get some people salivating even if there is not one to eat. Yet if one is allergic to gluten, Islamic or Jewish, or even merely vegetarian, this description may stir up entirely different feelings. Stories can evoke various emotions that may 'rub off' on the listener and lead to a change in mood. This may relate to specific fears or difficulties, or be oriented to more general changes in mood. For example, a story that illustrates how a protagonist overcomes a fear of failure and grows more confident may encourage a similar response in the client at an emotional level. From the perspective of cognitive psychotherapeutic models the personal meaning of events influences the clients' emotional and behavioural reactions. Stories, then, can be used to radically alter personal meanings of events and thus alter the kinds of emotional responses the client undergoes. Even in situations where a client does not share the same reality as the therapist a re-evaluation of events can evoke very different emotions. Close and Garety (1998) mention the case of an elderly woman whose primary diagnosis was schizophrenia. She was troubled by a sense of thought broadcasting and feared that all the rest of the congregation in the church she attended would ostracise her because of the obscene and lurid sexual thoughts that seemed to constantly fill her mind. Consequently, she went out far less and ceased attending church, and ended up living a much more restricted socially isolated life. However, she came to the understanding that as none of the other members of the congregation were behaving any differently towards her, they clearly were not too bothered by her thoughts and probably had similar ones themselves anyway. Thus she was far less distressed and able to resume her previous activities and lead a more interesting life.

Of course, not all fears are so florid or exotic. Mundane social anxieties are susceptible to this sort of approach too. The following anecdote, entitled 'What have you got to lose?', addresses the need to take a risk in challenging social anxiety and shyness to achieve emotional change. However, it does this by making the client identify with the person who appears to be coping better initially, before revealing how the less confident individual, who takes a risk, can receive far greater satisfaction.

'WHAT HAVE YOU GOT TO LOSE?'

Steve and Keith arranged to go to a nightclub to meet women. Steve was fairly confident about doing this. He planned what he would wear and what he might say to them. In contrast, Keith was inexperienced and anxious. So much so, that in the days leading up to the visit, he even contemplated feigning illness to get out of going. However, he went along despite his fears. At the club, Steve insisted that they approach two women at the bar and ask them for a dance. As Steve turned to approach them, Keith took a nervous step but hesitated, feeling extremely unsure of himself. At that point, he overheard a conversation and someone saying: 'What have you got to lose?'. The comment struck a chord with him and he knew immediately what he had to do. He took a deep breath, joined Steve, and talked to one of the women. He spent a happy evening chatting and dancing with her. At the end of the evening, she told Keith that she had a lovely time and agreed to go out the following night. In the taxi home, Keith told Steve how much he enjoyed the night, and doing something he found difficult to do. While Steve also had a good time, he hadn't done anything differently or been challenged. He hadn't experienced the excitement of risk and personal growth.

This kind of story works by using a kind of swap-over effect, whereby the person with the less helpful emotions learns to overcome them. This is a familiar story structure, which dates back at least to Shakespeare's time. Like Shakespeare's stories, it involves recognisable paradigms of desire, courage and romance. While not high art, this mundane tale of doing things differently to change our emotional lives may involve using quite simple forms of inspiration, often performed as a kind of ritual when faced with difficulties. The story above, needless to say, reflects a particular world view (Barker, 1989), and creates a kind of 'contract' with an implied reader or hearer. It represents a secular, hetero-sexual culture where men take the initiative in male–female relationships, and young men and women socialise together unsupervised. All of these features mean that the sorts of life experiences it talks about are exclusive to some extent. That is, people from different religious or cultural backgrounds and those with other sexual orientations might not find it so engaging. As such, the therapist might choose to adapt the story accordingly.

A number of further points relevant to chapter 2 on attitudes are illustrated by the story 'What have you got to lose?'. It highlights a principle of attitude change that has been discovered by a number of researchers (e.g. White et al., 2002), that as well as an attitude change message, the process is enhanced by exposure to a 'salient in-group'. That is, Keith's success is prompted by the messages he picks up from Steve's behaviour. Of course, not everyone wishes to play the heterosexual mating game. However, this story illustrates some of the feelings of hazard and uncertainty, which often accompany the transition to more satisfactory and fulfilling patterns of behaviour. A further feature is also worth noting. We are showing a kind of critical distance from the story. It is as if we, and the reader, are far too bright to be taken in by such a cliché. This, paradoxically, can make the story all the more effective, like the wooden horse that smuggled in the Greek soldiers. This sense of distance from the story is what some storytellers refer to as getting in front of the story, and making these kinds of remarks that show that they and the audience are cleverer – 'Well, you would, wouldn't you?'.

One of the authors was at a wedding recently when the vicar used exactly this technique to deliver his instructions regarding confetti: 'Now at this point, vicars usually say something about confetti, it's as if you've got to otherwise people think it's not a proper wedding and they're not properly married, so what this vicar says about confetti is …'. In 'getting in front' of his story, this particular vicar was clearly most effective for his instructions were obeyed to the letter and no confetti was dispensed until the happy couple and the wellwishers were at the churchyard gate, as instructed.

People seem to begin the process of developing preferences for certain kinds of stories and artefacts relatively early in life. Children identify stories as suitable for girls and boys almost as soon as they develop a sense of their own gender. Buckingham (1993) studied youngsters and cartoons. Among seven and eight year olds there seemed to be a strong sense that, for example, *Thundercats* 'ain't for girls', whereas *My little pony* was, even though the girls in the study were not interested in it. Girls tended to define themselves against cartoons, identifying them as 'for boys' and by extension as babyish and immature. The boys, especially the younger ones, were much more interested in celebrating their own preferences, such as displays of technology, violence and physical power. Another study of younger girls' preferences by Richards (in Buckingham, 1993) showed how some three and four year olds defined themselves as 'feminine' via a prefer-ence for particular stories and toys. This even extended to preferences for what they called 'girl colours' – pinks, mauves and pastels – as distinct from 'boy colours' – black, blue, orange and camouflage prints.

The implications of all this for storytelling in therapy are numerous. It highlights the importance of selecting stories on the basis of some shrewd guesses about the kinds of tale that will resonate with the client group in question. It may also give some clues as to where to start looking for stories that resonate. Many people can remember the stories, films and TV programmes they grew up with and these may form a point of departure for story construction. Some of us grew up with the popular *Dr Who* science fiction adventure series and, in time-honoured fashion, hid behind the sofa when things got scary. The silver-sprayed plywood Daleks with lethal weapons such as egg whisks and sink plungers protruding from their heads were not in themselves scary, but it was the creation of suspense through dialogue, music and scene setting that made them effective.

Whereas some stories create fear, there are many others that create a sense of wellbeing and social support. This is illustrated in the following anecdote with the double aim of revealing how a client is rarely alone in facing difficulties and providing a model 'ritual' that they themselves might wish to adopt when they are struggling to cope with a whole variety of fears.

'IN SPITE OF …'

A woman became depressed following a difficult divorce, which exacerbated chronic health problems. In the face of such difficulties she became very fearful about going out on her own, especially in crowded areas or brightly lit stores. Eventually she confided in her mother about her fears and her mother who listened carefully told her 'Hold on, I've got something that might help'. When she returned, she handed her daughter a scrap of paper on which were scribbled the words 'In spite of . . .'. When the daughter asked what this could possibly mean, the mother confided in her that she too had suffered from anxiety and depression as a young woman and that what had helped her through those tough times were these words. Whenever she had been fearful, she read the words over and over again. As her mother explained, the words conveyed that, in spite of everything, the future was open to positive change, hence the unfinished quality of the phrase. The daughter was genuinely surprised by her mother's admission, since she had always seemed a confident and relaxed person. With the scrap of paper to read when she needed to, the daughter drew courage to face up to and gradually overcome her fear of going out alone.

Since the feeling of happiness is a major preventative of so many negative states, such as depression, anxiety, phobias and relationship difficulties, any kind of anecdote that provides this kind of message is welcome in therapeutic contexts. As well as providing a kind of ritual and mantra to help deal with negative feelings, it also illustrates how people can support one another. The process of caring for a loved one with a mental health problem is widely acknowledged to be an exhausting process (Jeon & Madjar, 1998). While many therapists, counsellors and even nurses can go off duty, the role of a parent in such circumstances can be difficult indeed. In this anecdote, then, another important feature is modelled. The sharing of experience in a respectful and non-demanding way can be valuable. It shows, from the point of view of the client, how an apparently small item can mean a great deal. In a sense it also demonstrates the use of these items of support such that clients can create positive emotions such as happiness or courage themselves, without having to rely too heavily on others to supply them.

Whereas it is often useful to clients to have robust, supportive social networks, sometimes it is equally the case that people might benefit from developing a greater degree of independence and self reliance. One of the authors once worked with a client who was severely phobic and who needed constant company and reassurance to perform many everyday tasks. Her life was becoming increasingly restricted and she was doing less and less. As this woman was emotionally quite fragile it was felt important not to alienate her in therapy so an animal story was used to make the story less threatening to her. The story was about a young monkey who would cling to the safety of his mother or any other monkey in his troop instead of exploring the forest and having fun with his peers. He would cling on to his mother's hand for safety and if this was prised off he'd use his very dextrous feet. He'd sometimes even use his long prehensile tail.

Following on from this story it might be possible to discuss what exactly the monkey might be missing out on, and what might happen to him if he remained attached to his mother. It might be possible to use ideas like this also in a kind of guided imagery technique, such that a range of positive images and experiences can be attached to being independent and exploring the social world. This, then, can be used to help overcome the fear of being on one's own, because there are all kinds of more exciting things to do. To make this effective we might begin by inviting the client to think of things that might happen if, for example, they were able to go out. They might think about being able to go to work, go shopping and begin a search for a romantic partner. Once these images are firmly visualised the client can think of how good all these things would feel. The images and the feelings can be strung together so that the client can play them in their head like a movie. In a sense also this technique is like a rosary where each bead has a prayer attached. The sequence of images can be 'played back' by the client whenever necessary, and may even eclipse the fear and dread attached to going out of the house. In a sense, they might also act as a motor to enhance change.

In dealing with emotions in therapy we have noted that many accounts from clients of unpleasant emotions emphasise how the emotional episodes can appear suddenly and seem to have great power, which takes over and leaves the client with little control. Anger episodes, panic attacks and mood swings often appear in this way. The physiological changes that occur during emotional experiences and which help energise us for any action needed form part of what Walter Cannon (1927; 1942) called the 'fight or flight response'. The physical changes may be subtle at first and we may only become aware of them by the time they are intense or out of our control. This is because our attention is focused with the cognitions that trigger them. It is therefore useful to train oneself to be able to shift one's attention away from the trigger to the physiological changes themselves at their earliest manifestation.

With clients who have difficulty managing their intense emotions, such as anger problems, we can employ Dwivedi's (1997) analogy of catching snakes to emphasise the importance of intervening early on in the anger process. To a client who is having difficulties with sudden 'attacks' of emotion, such as one person we recall who was showing a good deal of verbal aggression and destroying a good deal of property, we might ask, 'Have you ever watched someone catching snakes?'. The client may look a bit puzzled at this point. Then we can continue along the lines of: 'Well, it is virtually impossible once they are loose. They move so fast in unexpected directions and there is nothing to grab hold of. However, it is possible if you wait for the snakes to emerge from their holes in the ground. As they initially poke their head up it offers an opportunity to catch them with a forked stick fairly easily.'

Often stories don't need further elaboration but it can be useful to make a more explicit link to the client, such as 'anger is a bit like that'. If the client can learn to recognise early their anger symptoms they stand a far better chance at managing them, because anger tends to build up in intensity over time. Early management may involve learning and implementing techniques such as breathing, relaxation exercises and cognitive self soothing, in order to break the anger cycle and increase the likelihood of avoiding intense, disabling emotions.

The initial question 'Have you ever watched someone catch snakes?' in itself has a novelty aspect that makes it quite memorable. This analogy could be further utilised on a cue card for a client to read prior to entering a potentially anger provoking situation, such as 'remember catching snakes' as a reminder that we stand a better chance of controlling our emotions if we act before they get out of hand.

Another useful story identified by Dwivedi (1997) highlights one aspect of the process of paradoxical intention, where the client is encouraged to do the opposite of what feels 'natural' in order to combat undesired emotions. This particular example is useful to employ in relation to anger. This story comes from the Buddhist book, *Samyutta Nikaya*.

AN ANGER-EATING DEMON

An anger-eating demon thrived on people becoming angry. The demon, therefore, went around annoying people and making them angry. Once he went to the 'plane of 33 gods', gatecrashed up to the throne of the king of the gods and deposited himself on it. The king, Sakka, was away at the time. When the other gods found out they were furious with the demon. The more they became angry, the more the demon grew bigger, shining and bright. When Sakka arrived, the gods informed him of what was going on. Sakka, therefore, approached the demon with great humility, without any sign of anger, prostrated himself in front of the demon three times and appeared most welcoming. Thus, the anger-eating demon was starved of feeding on any anger and could not survive. He kept on shrinking until he became negligible and went somewhere else in search of people whom he could make angry and whose anger he could relish (Dwivedi, 1997, p. 97).

The above story conveys important features of several anger management strategies, which also resonate with a number of cognitive behavioural techniques. We may encourage clients to think of ways in which they are 'feeding' their own anger-eating demon, i.e. excessive rumination on anger evoking events, creating an unhelpful internal dialogue full of 'musts' and 'shoulds'. By considering doing the opposite of raising one's anger, it might highlight how the angry feelings have emerged in the first place, what implicit moral code has been violated and that some person has been blamed to create the episode.

Cross-cultural research suggests that some cultures, such as the Inuit, lack anger, according to Solomon (1984), because they do not blame individuals for their actions. They feel annoyed and even act violently, yet this is not equivalent to anger. Solomon takes pains to describe how the Inuit do not merely suppress anger; they appear not to feel it either. Animals and human infants also do not feel anger per se because they lack a concept of personal responsibility. They can feel upset, disturbed, threatened and aggressive, but not angry at someone for what they have done.

This peculiar interplay between highly acculturated systems of values, ethics and moralities and the allegedly more primitive levels of fight and flight are the central paradoxes of emotion. As Vygotsky said 'the brain systems directly linked to affective functions have an extremely unique organization. They are the lowest, most ancient, most primary systems of the brain, and the highest, most recent, and most specific human structure' (Vygotsky, 1987, p. 85).

When therapists talk about strategies of thinking to combat emotions, these often involve analogies with action or are phrased in terms of action words. Phrases like thought stopping, thought blocking or counter-attacking emphasise this especially. As McMullin (2000) notes, hard countering is an emotional process as well as an intellectual one. Therapists can pair emotions with beliefs, and they can use their clients' strong emotions to change beliefs directly. One analogy to explain to clients how strong emotions can help them change their damaging beliefs, is what McMullin (2000) calls the 'Melted Wax Theory':

> Consider, for a moment, that thoughts are like wax impressions in your brain. They are often formed when we have a strong emotion like fear or anger. These emotions act on your thoughts like heat, causing them to liquefy and reform into new beliefs. When the heat of high emotional arousal has dissipated, the thought is solidified. To change the belief you have to either chip away at the wax impression, which takes a long time, or reheat the wax so the thought can be remolded. If you get angry and assertive enough with irrational thoughts, it is like heating them up so that they can be poured into a new mold.

(p. 92)

Now, of course, few brain scientists would support this model of the brain. That isn't the point. The beauty of this story is that it puts a positive gloss on some of the otherwise dispiriting conflicts and self directed anger that may emerge as clients struggle with beliefs and emotions they wish to change. As McMullin notes, the key aspect in disputing unhelpful thoughts or beliefs is the expression of 'emotion in a high state of arousal', which 'virtually eliminates the repetitious, mechanical parroting that so often renders counters ineffectual' (p. 92).

The apparently overwhelming feelings that constitute emotions can sometimes prompt rash actions. The story of the 'puzzling suicide' from Dwivedi's (1997) collection can serve as a warning about acting rashly or being overwhelmed by small setbacks. Here the formerly blind man who had his sight restored killed himself when the train on which he was travelling went through a tunnel and he misinterpreted this as a return of his blindness. Even if we have experienced some improvement we – and, more importantly, clients – must expect to go through tunnels. No matter how long they seem to be, we will eventually come out the other side, back to the light.

Even when clients can be persuaded that they can challenge their unhelpful or dysfunctional beliefs when they are calm, they often say that they simply do not believe or access them when they are distressed. Like Ellis noted 40 years earlier, the emotional insight may be lacking. Either clients cannot bring to mind the new thoughts at the crucial time or they simply do not believe them. The alternative thoughts – depression, anger or panic - seem far more compelling.

Paul Gilbert (2000), in his work on cognitive behaviour therapy for depression, notes how depressive thinking, when a person is at their most depressed, is compelling, persuasive, vivid, well established and self fulfilling, whereas more functional, less depressed thinking may be new, weak, unconvincing, and therefore readily forgotten and rapidly abandoned in the face of apparently overwhelming despair. Gilbert (2000) uses a computer program analogy to explain why this may be so, in that it resembles plugging in one cassette or computer program at one time, and using another at another time, but without there being any interaction between the two. The analogy is that no matter how rational a client's thinking is, it will not necessarily transfer across from a non-depressed to a depressed state – the two 'programs' are entirely separate. The client has to be in the depressed 'program' to learn to incorporate new thinking within it. There are two components to the procedure Gilbert suggests – re-experiencing the emotional episode and mood induction. In this way a small dose of the negative emotion can be induced in the clinical setting and clients can practise banishing it with whatever newly learned techniques are at their disposal. Perhaps over time, by a process of classical conditioning, the negative emotion will come to evoke the techniques for defusing it.

This kind of technique emphasises a kind of graduated exposure to the negative emotions and moods, and a gradual process of practising the cognitive skills necessary for disarming it. On the other hand sometimes the moment of therapeutic change takes place as a result of an experience of 'flooding' where a high intensity experience induces a sudden change. For example, the following story, from McMullin (2000), illustrates such a moment in the life of one young man.

THE STORY OF DANIEL

Daniel was a person who feared going crazy, and this fear dominated his life. He was afraid that someday his emotions (particularly tension and anxiety) would become so powerful that they would make him go crazy. He wasn't sure exactly how stress could make one's brain snap, but he was certain it could happen. He vividly pictured himself locked in a padded cell, confined in a straitjacket, lying in the back ward of a dirty, broken-down, mental hospital, screaming day after day, month after month, with nobody in the world giving a dam [sic]. It terrified him.

He did everything he could imagine to avoid losing his mind. He visited a dozen doctors, tried all kinds of tranquilizers and avoided watching any movie or TV show or reading any novel that discussed insane people. He tried to keep his fear from escalating by living alone in his house so that others couldn't upset him. He spent most of his day watching mild sitcoms on TV. He didn't like them, but at least they didn't make him afraid.

Still, no matter what he tried he would still occasionally get anxious, and when that happened he would rush to the phone and call his therapist, demanding admission to the local hospital. There he would be sedated until the fear went away. He'd had himself admitted 5 times in two years.

Late one winter night Daniel was lying on the couch with the TV on, half asleep but still vaguely aware of the sights and sounds around him. Suddenly he started to feel anxious. He sat up, concerned, and looked around for a cause. Finally he noticed that the TV was tuned to a talk show about ex-mental patients who were describing their experiences in full and gory detail. He quickly got up and changed the channel, but it was too late; he had heard too much. He was unable to block his fear, and it quickly grew into a full-fledged panic attack.

He tried everything he could to reduce it. He rushed to his medicine cabinet to take some tranquilizers, but the bottle was empty. He remembered he had hidden a reserve bottle in case he ever ran out, but he'd forgotten where it was. He rummaged desperately through all the cabinets, closets, and boxes in his apartment, but he couldn't find them anywhere.

He went to emergency plan #2. Despite the late hour, he called his therapist but found no answer, then remembered that he was out of town. He tried phoning some of his past therapists, but reached answering machines or found that their phones had been disconnected. He tried calling two different 24-hour crisis lines, but both told him not to worry about it. He scrambled for someone else to call, knowing that though he had lost his friends through the years, he still had some relatives who might help. He phoned them and woke them up, but after years of hearing Daniel cry wolf, they were tired of his panics. They didn't appreciate being woken up in the middle of the night, and told him he would have to handle the problem himself.

His fears rising to a maximum, he rushed out of the house, jumped into his car and drove as fast as he could to the emergency room of the county hospital. But when he arrived he found that there had been an ice blizzard on one of the major freeways and twenty-five cars had been involved in a pile-up. The hospital staff were running around trying to help the accident victims and he was told that they didn't have time to see him.

So there he was – trapped. He had no place to go, no one to call, nobody to turn to. Deciding that since he was going to panic he might as well do it at home, he got into his car and drove back to his apartment. He sat in his living room chair, turned the lights off, and waited for his brain to snap and to go insane. He sat there for two hours, letting the waves of panic flow over him. Later on Daniel described what had happened to him as he sat waiting. (This dialogue is reconstructed from his report.)

'I was sitting there with waves and waves of panic, exhausted, terrified, with no place to go and no-one to turn to. I was waiting to go crazy. But suddenly out of nowhere, I jumped up and started to talk to myself out loud. I talked louder and louder until I was shouting at myself. I said, "Who the hell cares if I go insane? It couldn't be any worse than what I'm feeling now. My life hasn't been worth a bucket of shit for the last 10 years. I'm not married, I don't have girlfriends, I can't hold a job, and I've been on medical disability for the last 10 years. I have no friends, my relatives can't stand me, and my therapists are tired of me. So who the hell cares? This isn't a life. I don't have to fear losing anything, because there is nothing left to lose. There is no reason to protect myself anymore. It doesn't matter what precautions I take – they don't work, so what difference does it make? I've had it. The hell with it all. If I'm going to go insane, I'm going to go insane, but

I'm not going to escape anymore. There is no place to escape to, anyway. If I'm ultimately going to end up a loony, I might just as well have a good time before I do!'"

Afterwards he got up, walked out of the house and went to an all night restaurant where he had the biggest, gooiest pizza he could find. He ate the whole thing, then went to an all-night movie and didn't return home until dawn.

This was Daniel's turning point. Having been faced with a crisis from which there was no escape, Daniel chose an alternative B and he never looked back. His panics subsided, and he tried to live life to the fullest. He began to travel and took some classes in school. He looked for a job and started to date. Some time later he found his hidden pills, but immediately threw them away in disgust. At the end of the year he was a totally different person and almost never got anxious. All of this can be traced back to that winter night when he chose to break through his dam.'

(McMullin, 2000, pp. 106–9)

Another story along similar lines is 'Thief in the night':

THIEF IN THE NIGHT

There was a man called Charlie, who couldn't sleep for fear of dying. Sleep itself seemed the most likely state for this to occur, and thus he propped open his eyes into the early hours, or even until the next day. Previously, Charlie had been very fit and healthy, and was unlikely to suffer any terminal physical collapse. After all, he was only 25 years old! But his fear of dying was taking its toll on his system. His work suffered for the lack of sleep, so much so that his manager had complained about his performance. Even his girlfriend grew tired of his moodiness during the day. He was beginning to look pale and older than his years. But one night, while lying in bed, with his eyes wide open, Charlie had a break-through in his thinking. It took the shape of a brief argument with the figure of Death. Frustrated by the decline in his fitness for work and relationships, he cried out: 'Death, you can take me, but you're not having my sleep as well!' This brief response was like a magic key that opened his thinking to a measured and healthier response. From that night on he slept soundly and the 'thief in the night' left empty-handed.

A story that can be used with clients with obsessive compulsive disorder is 'The rabbit and the black box'. For example, a client who constantly checks electrical equipment and security items like locks on doors and windows in his house, to prevent accidents or misfortunes happening (events that he would hold himself responsible for) may be helped by this adapted anonymous story.

THE RABBIT AND THE BLACK BOX

One day a rabbit was crossing the road when he got his foot caught in a drain in the road. He was frantically pulling at his leg and a car was rapidly approaching. He thought it was his end when he was suddenly released and snatched to safety by a man who had observed his predicament. The rabbit was so grateful to the man that he granted him a wish. The man thought hard and said 'I'd like a really nice house'. True to his word the rabbit took him to a fabulous mansion within beautiful grounds. Just before leaving, the man noticed that there was a large black box in one of the bedrooms. He asked the rabbit about it. The rabbit warned him just not to open it and with that left him alone. The man moved his stuff into the new house and couldn't believe his good fortune in meeting the rabbit, but then he started to have a niggling thought about what might happen if he got drunk and flung open the box. To prevent this happening he got rid of all his drink and felt better. But then he thought, but what if a visitor became curious and looked inside, so he stopped having people round and locked the door. But then he wondered what might happen if someone broke in while he was away from the house so he rarely went out and topped up all his security. As the years went by more and more of the house was locked up to make it secure until he was actually living in one room in the house and sleeping in his armchair with a weapon at hand in case anyone broke in. One day he reluctantly visited his doctor. The doctor told him he had an incurable disease and had only hours to live. He knew exactly what he would do. He rushed home, threw open all the locks, went up to the bedroom and flung upon the big black box. He looked inside and found nothing. He waited and do you know what happened? Absolutely nothing.

Similarities can be drawn between the story and the client's life. That is, the client is not really living but is spending all her life worrying about something that may never happen.

In working with a client with difficulties managing their anger it may be helpful for them to consider the self destructiveness of their anger.

NAILING ANGER

There was a boy who frequently got angry. His father gave him a big bag of nails and told him that every time he lost his temper, to hammer as many nails as he could into the tree at the bottom of the garden. The first day the boy had driven 50 nails into its trunk. Then it gradually dwindled down in number. He discovered it was easier to hold his temper than to drive those nails into the tree. Finally the day came when the boy didn't lose his temper at all. He told his father about it and the father suggested that the boy now pull out one nail for each day that he was able to hold his temper. The days passed and the young boy was finally able to tell his father that all the nails were gone. The father took his son by the hand and led him to the tree. He said, 'Now look at the holes in this tree and think of it as you. When you get angry, you hurt and scar yourself, just as you have wounded this tree'.

Adapted from Author Unknown

Maybe it is helpful to remember the destructive nature of negative emotion, and that it's more about 'losing the battle to win the war'.

A useful tale, which can remind us of our responsibility for how we feel, and that we have to learn ways of managing our emotions and not letting them manage us, is the anonymous tale, 'The wolves'. It may be useful for clients who have a tendency to blame others for their misfortune. The story is as follows:

THE WOLVES

A father was teaching his son about anger. 'It is like there are two wolves inside of us,' he said. 'The one is good and does no harm, living in harmony with everyone. The other is full of anger. Anything will set him off into a rage, even though this response does him no good in the end. It is hard to live with these two wolves inside of us.' The boy thought for a while and asked his father, 'Which one wins?'. His father, smiling, told him, 'The one we choose to feed'.

Another anonymous story to adopt with people who bear a grudge or dwell on injustices is 'Letting go'.

LETTING GO

There was once a shopkeeper in a small town who had identical twin sons, John and Tom. The boys worked for their father in the store he owned and, when he died, they took it over. Everything went well until the day a five pound note disappeared. John had left the money on the cash register and walked outside with a customer. When he returned, the money was gone. He asked his brother, 'Did you see that five pounds on the cash register?'. Tom replied that he had not. But John kept probing and questioning. He would not let it alone. 'Money just doesn't get up and walk away! Surely you must have seen it!' There was subtle accusation in his voice. Tempers began to rise. Resentment set in. Before long, a deep and bitter chasm divided the young men. They refused to speak. They finally decided they could no longer work together and a dividing wall was built down the centre of the store. For 20 years hostility and bitterness grew, spreading to their families and to the community. Then one day a man drove his car up to the front of the store. He walked in and asked one of the brothers, 'How long have you been here?'. John replied that he'd been there all his life. The customer said, 'I must share something with you. Twenty years ago I was homeless and desperate and I hadn't eaten for days. I came into this store from the back door and saw a five pound note on the cash register. I put it in my pocket and walked out. All these years I haven't been able to forget that. I know it wasn't much money, but I had to come back and ask your forgiveness.' The stranger was amazed to see tears well up in the eyes of this middle-aged man.

'Would you please go next door and tell that same story to my brother on the other side of the store?' he said. After he did this, the man was even more amazed to see two middle-aged men, who looked very much alike, embracing each other and weeping together. After 20 years, the brokenness was mended. The wall of resentment that had divided them came down.

It is so often the little things that finally divide people: words spoken in haste; criticisms; accusations; resentments. And once divided, they may never come together again. The solution, of course, is to let it go. There is really nothing particularly profound about learning to let go of little resentments. But for fulfilling and lasting relationships, letting them go is a must. Refuse to carry around bitterness and you may be surprised at how much energy you have left for building bonds with those you love. The issue of letting go has also taken its place in the repertoire of popular psychology, and many successful paperbacks on self help and self image improvement emphasise this aspect. For all that, it is still valuable. There is a growing body of research to suggest that forgiveness is thera-peutic. For example, Karremans et al. (2003) discovered that forgiving was associated with enhanced wellbeing, especially in committed relationships. Forgiving someone to whom one has been close seems to offer greater increases in wellbeing than someone who is a relative stranger.

A current incarnation of behavioural theories in clinical practice is Linehan's (1993) work in the treatment of so-called borderline personality disorders. Linehan's theoretical perspective is consistent with the experiential theories (primary and secondary emotions), and as such does not fall within the radical behaviourist tradition. However, its clinical principles are fundamentally behaviourist and consist of teaching more adaptive skills, including the skills of observation and regulation of affect. 'Much of the borderline individual's emotional distress is a result of secondary responses (e.g. intense shame, anxiety, or rage) to primary emotions. Often the primary emotions are adaptive and appropriate to the context. The reduction of this secondary distress requires exposure to the primary emotion in a nonjudgmental atmosphere' (Linehan, 1993, p. 84). One of the key methods in treatment is the use of Zen-inspired mindfulness skills, that is, refined skills of observations of internal emotional, cognitive and physical states. This in itself is interesting from the point of view of this chapter as there is a tradition of telling allegories and stories in Zen teaching as a way of developing the self and ideas about consciousness. For example, the often intractable patterns of emotional turmoil from which these clients suffer, especially in response to abusive or confusing experiences, can be likened to calluses, like those on a violinist's fingers, which develop with long hours of using an instrument, which help their bearer to adapt to his or her tools. Some changes in our selves may be reversible. The calluses on the violi-nist's fingers cannot be reasoned away, but they may disappear if she fails to practise. However they will return when she spends sufficient time with her instrument once more. Such physical calluses are easily understood, and they arise from a human being's interaction with his or her environment and tools.

This 'emotional callusing' process is also believed to be one of the issues at stake in 'survivor guilt', experienced by those who are involved in some trauma or tragedy and who continue to undergo the repercussions of the experience for some time afterwards (Matsakis, 1999). The senses of empathy, compassion and concern for friends, relatives and people with whom one is connected is somehow enlisted into the memory of the experience and yields the guilt. In many contexts, the possibility of guilt protects us from undertaking actions that might be rash, and it prompts us to avoid or make amends for socially or ethically inappropriate actions. However, in some cases this adaptive and socially impor-tant feeling cannot help us, in a sense because the worst has already happened. Survivors of disasters, accidents, warfare or the Nazi Holocaust have often been troubled by 'survivor guilt'. The work of Leo Montada (1996) has a bearing on this point. This kind of guilt, he reasoned, arises when, for example, a person is the sole survivor of an accident, or escapes persecution or survives a concentra-tion camp. Primo Levi was so consumed by this pervading sense of guilt, having lived through the Holocaust as an Italian Jew, that he committed suicide decades later. This feeling is easy to understand when the survivor was close to those who perished. Montada wanted to know if such guilt is also felt in less extreme circumstances and whether it is experienced in regard to socially distant indivi-duals or strangers. He found that three factors were necessary to produce such guilt: they accepted the fact that there were people less fortunate than themselves; they believed that the needy were not deserving of their fate; and they believed that their wellbeing was linked to another's misfortune. Thus, the guilt they experienced motivated them to take action on behalf of the needy. In other words, those who felt guilt already had a set of ethical values. This, then, is a further example of the point we made earlier – that the presence of emotions is bound up with sets of values, moral judgements and ethical systems. Whereas we may not be aware of these, considering somewhat more extreme disasters in this way might help expose not only a client's half submerged sense of guilt, but help to defuse it. A friend of one of the authors had been troubled during her adult life with repeated bouts of self directed rage. This had been sufficiently puzzling and severe to have landed her with the diagnosis of 'personality disorder' at one stage. Whereas she freely shared the fact that she had suffered a most unhappy childhood, further aspects of these feelings emerged by comparison with the notion of survivor guilt. She eventually formulated some of her difficulties as being to do with the fact that her siblings had fared less well than she had. One of her sisters had died under mysterious circumstances in childhood and, while nothing was ever proved, my friend believed this was due to maltreatment at the hands of the parents. Her other sister and brother had also been abused and had undergone periods of psychiatric treatment. In a sense she regarded herself as the 'one who had escaped', yet this brought with it a sense of guilt that the others had not succeeded in doing so.

Thus, in this chapter we hope to have made an effective plea for therapists to consider the use of stories and anecdotes where it is appropriate to change emotions that may be causing the client distress. The advantages are especially apparent when we consider the way that researchers and practitioners throughout much of the twentieth century and beyond have noted that reason and cognitive reorientations alone cannot tackle some of the more clinically significant emotions we will encounter. The very fact that stories work indirectly and are allusive rather than direct can be advantageous under these circumstances. Ellis's early frustration that emotional understanding did not necessarily follow from cognitive understanding can be addressed in this way. Finally, it is worth noting the use of 'stories' of one sort or another was a prominent part at the very outset of modern-day psychotherapy around a hundred years ago. Both Freud and Jung drew heavily on classical mythology to make sense of the peculiar modes of action of their clients' anxieties, and both used stories or narratives as vehicles for undertaking therapeutic work. Whether these were derived from clients' own dreams or from mythology and religions around the world, these tales were central to the creation of many of our present day notions of how the mind works.

REFERENCES

Ang, I. (1985) *Watching Dallas. Soap opera and the melodramatic imagination*. London: Methuen.

Averill, J. (1980) A constructionist view of emotion. In R. Plutchik & H. Kellerman (Eds.). *Emotion: Theory, research, and experience* (Volume 1). New York: Academic Press.

Barker, M. (1989) *Comics: Ideology, power and the critics*. Manchester: Manchester University Press.

Buckingham, D. (1993) *Reading audiences*. Manchester: Manchester University Press.

Burns, G. W. (2001) *101 healing stories: Using metaphors in therapy*. New York and Chichester: John Wiley & Sons.

Cannon, W. B. (1927) The James-Lange theory of emotion. *American Journal of Psychology*, **39**, 106–24.

Cannon, W. B. (1942) Voodoo death. *American Anthropologist*, **44**, 169–81.

Close, H. & Garety, P. (1998) Cognitive assessment of voices: Further developments in understanding the emotional impact of voices. *British Journal of Clinical Psychology*, **37**, 173–88.

Dwivedi, K. N. (Ed.)(1997) *The therapeutic use of stories*. London: Routledge.

Ellis, A. (1963) *Reason and emotion in psychotherapy*. New York: Lyle Stuart.

Ellis, A. & Dryden, W. (1997) *The practice of rational-emotive behaviour therapy*. New York: Springer Publishing Company, Inc.

Gilbert, P. (2000) *Overcoming depression. A self-help guide using cognitive behavioural techniques*. London: Robinson.

Harre, R. & Gillett, G. (1994) *The discursive mind*. London: Sage.

Heller, M. B. (1993) The rime of the papyraceous twin. *British Journal of Psychotherapy*, **10**(1), 18–25.

Hollway, W. (1984) Gender difference and the production of subjectivity. In J. Henriques, W. Hollway, C. Venn & V. Walkerdine (Eds.). *Changing the subject*. London: Methuen.

Hollway, W. (1989) *Subjectivity and method in psychology*. London: Sage.

Izard, C. E. (1984) Emotion–cognition relationships and human development. In C. E. Izard,

J. Kagan & R. B. Zajonc (Eds.). *Emotions, cognitions and behaviour*. New York: Cambridge University Press.

Izard, C. & Buechler, S. (1980) Aspects of consciousness and personality in terms of differential emotions theory. In R. Plutchik & H. Kellerman, (Eds.). *Emotion: Theory, research, and experience* (volume 1, chapter 7). New York: Academic Press.

Jeon, Y. H. & Madjar, I. (1998) Caring for a family member with chronic mental illness. *Qualitative Health Research*, 8(5), 694–706.

Karremans, J. C., Van Lange, P. A. M., Ouwerkerk, J. W. & Kluwer, E. R. S. (2003) When forgiving enhances psychological wellbeing: The role of interpersonal commitment. *Journal of Personality and Social Psychology*, 84(5), 1011–26.

Linehan, M. (1993) *Cognitive behavioural treatment of borderline personality disorder*. New York: Guilford Press.

Matsakis, A. (1999) *Survivor guilt*. Oakland, Calif.: New Harbinger Publications Inc.

McMullin, R. E. (2000) *The new handbook of cognitive therapy techniques*. New York and London: W. W. Norton & Company.

Montada, L. (1996) *Current societal concerns about justice*. New York: Kluwer Academic Publishers.

Sarbin, T. R. (1987) Emotion and act: Roles and rhetoric. In R. Harre (Ed.). *The social construction of emotions*. Oxford: Basil Blackwell.

Schacter, S. & Singer, J. E. (1962) Cognitive, social and physiological determinants of emotional state. *Psychological Review*, **69**, 379–99.

Solomon, R. C. (1984) Emotions and choice. In A. Rorty (Ed.). *Explaining emotions* (chapter 10). Berkeley: University of California Press.

Stearns, C. Z. & Stearns, P. (1986) *Anger: The struggle for emotional control in America's history*. Chicago: University of Chicago Press.

Stearns, P. & Lewis, J. (1998) *An emotional history of the United States*. New York: New York University Press.

Trower, P., Casey, A. & Dryden, W. (1988) *Cognitive-behavioural counselling in action*. London: Sage.

Vygotsky, L. S. (1987, originally published 1934) Thinking and speech. In R. W. Rieber & A. S. Carton (Eds.). *The collected works of L. S. Vygotsky*. Volume 1. Problems of General Psychology. Including the volume Thinking and Speech. 37–285. London: Plenum Press.

White, K. M., Hogg, M. A. & Terry, D. A., (2002) Improving attitude behaviour correspondence through exposure to normative support from a salient in-group. *Basic and Applied Social Psychology*, **24**(2), 91–103.

Zajonc, R. B. (1980) Feeling and thinking: Preferences need no inferences. *American Psychologist*, **35**, 151–75.

Zajonc, R. B. (1984) On the primacy of affect. *American Psychologist*, **39**, 117–23.

4 BEHAVIOUR CHANGE

A common goal in therapy is changing unhelpful patterns of behaviour. Very often, in exploring the kinds of goals people have for themselves these are expressed in terms of 'doing' words: 'I'd like to be able to talk to people at parties' or 'I wish I could go shopping without having panic attacks'. The desired changes in behaviour might be at varying levels of complexity. For example, the therapist may be working together with the client to generally improve social confidence or overcome a severe and disabling anxiety disorder. The point is that many of the objectives of therapy are about being able to do new things, resume desired activities or give up doing things that might be dysfunctional.

For example, in avoidance-type behaviours, people might panic when coming face to face with feared objects. This might involve a number of self imposed restrictions, such as withdrawing from society or failing to speak due to anxiety. On the other hand, some behaviour becomes problematic because people indulge in it excessively. At the present time the mass media are full of examples of 'approach behaviours' that are problematic. As well as the usual ones such as alcohol, drug and gambling problems a variety of novel approach behaviours have been identified as causing problems in recent years, such as compulsive shopping, compulsive internet use and compulsive sexuality. In everyday parlance, these are often described as, for example, internet addiction and sex addiction, and especially in the United States a great many treatment programmes have been developed using the Alcoholics Anonymous approach.

All these difficulties, then, involve a strong desire on the part of professionals and clients to induce some change in behaviour. One intuitively reasonable assumption has been that to change people's behaviour you need to change their attitudes. This kind of approach has been a cornerstone of many psychological interventions, for example, in changing health behaviour (Rutter & Quine, 2002) and in psychotherapy (Keijsers, 1999). It is assumed that if you make people feel that a course of action is a good idea, whether it be giving up smoking or challenging anxieties, then the desired behaviour will follow.

This assumption does not always turn out to be true. Attitudinal and cognitive factors do not always correspond to behaviour (Ajzen, 2000). That is why we are devoting a whole chapter to behaviour in its own right. Moreover, despite the commonsense assumption that attitudes, thoughts and feelings determine behaviour, there are many examples in the last half century of psychology of exactly the opposite occurring. Sometimes behaviour seems to influence attitudes, thoughts and feelings. The classic work of Festinger and Carlsmith (1959) is well known. In their original study, participants were paid to say that a boring task was in fact interesting. Those who were paid a large, twenty dollar fee (equivalent to a week's wages in the late 1950s) still felt the task was boring. Those paid a small, one dollar fee apparently changed their minds about the task and decided it must have been more interesting. This was allegedly because of 'dissonance'. People were uncomfortable at telling lies for such a small amount of money, so they reinterpreted the situation and decided that what they said was true. Cognitions and attitudes, then, follow behaviour. Over the ensuing half century there were many more classic examples of this phenomenon. For instance, Hobden and Olson (1994) had people read 'lawyer jokes' into a tape recorder. Those who believed they were doing so voluntarily showed more attitude change (towards disliking lawyers) than those who felt they had been coerced. The attitude change effect will also be stronger if the participants believe that someone important will be listening or reading the results, and be able to identify you. For example, Leippe and Eisenstadt's (1994) participants had to advocate a policy favourable to another race. If they felt they could be identified and held responsible they apparently felt more favourable towards the policy and the racial group. Dissonance may explain why people tend to rate their decisions more favourably after they have made them. Brehm (1956) demonstrated this with people choosing domestic appliances. Knox and Inkster (1968) noted that after people had placed a bet they were more optimistic about their horses than before they betted. Younger et al. (1977) found people placed more confidence in their chosen candidate after voting in an election than before.

There are many therapeutic implications of this kind of work. If you can get people to do something, you are often well on the way to changing their attitudes and cognitions. As long ago as 1890 William James said 'Sit all day in a melancholy posture, sigh and reply to everything with a dismal voice and your melancholy lingers' (James, 1890, p. 43).

Sometimes externally imposed changes in behaviour can have a therapeutic effect too. For example, an acquaintance of one of the authors developed financial difficulties while at university and he began to check his bank balance regularly via cashpoint machines. This became increasingly frequent. From once a day it became several times a day and he would sometimes have to sneak out of lectures to check to see if particular transactions had been processed. This became more and more disabling as his rising sense of anxiety and agitation could only be assuaged by checking his balance. Routes to go to the shops had to be planned so as to pass cashpoints linked to his bank. Some of us wondered whether he would ever survive in the world outside, or even manage to sit through a three hour finals examination. However, he landed a rather enviable job at a research centre in a converted stately home, miles from any cashpoints. We wondered how he would cope, but in the end he did not seem to have too many difficulties. Here, the externally imposed change in the protagonist's life circumstances led to changes in attitudes, behaviour and, presumably also, his anxiety levels. While we do not exactly know what he was feeling, the constraints on his behaviour might well have helped to reconfigure his emotional life. In a sense, when people are induced to behave in a particular manner they might be saying to themselves something like 'Well, I'm doing this and it's not too bad'.

This use of induced change in behaviour to make a difference to clients was famously exploited by Lewinsohn, beginning in the 1970s to treat depression. His strategy was one of *reintroducing pleasurable events*. This begins with the client completing schedules of pleasant events and selecting a set of these that the client is then encouraged to do each week by means of a 'contract'. There is some evidence that this does indeed lead to greater participation in the activities and an improved mood (Teri & Lewinsohn, 1986). Moreover, in studies by Schlenker et al. (1994) and Tice (1992), when people were induced to act in a talkative, outgoing manner they were more inclined to perceive themselves as outgoing and the behaviour persisted after the experiment was over. In addition, the example of the friend who recovered from his 'cashpoint addiction' demonstrates a further point that some researchers have begun to identify. Starting a new job is an example of what has been called a 'fresh start' experience. These many also take the form of a new romantic relationship, a new project or a change of residence. Harris et al. (1999) have documented the role of these 'fresh starts' in relieving depression in women. Again, the message here is that once a change in behaviour has been induced, positive emotional consequences can ensue. Everyday phrases like 'I need a break' and 'getting away from it all' encapsulate an important truth.

This impetus to change behaviour can be enhanced through the use of stories, metaphors or anecdotes, which are especially useful when they provide a ready vehicle for describing preferred or desired behaviours. Through repetition, such examples of desired 'goal behaviours' can influence clients and change the way they respond in certain situations. This approach may be sufficiently gentle and non-threatening to avoid resistance from the client who may be tired of having their negative behaviour challenged directly. The client can have a model of the ideal behaviour that may positively influence their behaviour. Through carefully chosen stories, clients may be able to adopt positive behavioural goals such as accepting help from others, expressing anger, self control, being more assertive, setting limits, mixing with others socially and limiting self criticism.

As Dwivedi (1997) notes, developing habitual responses may mean that they are used in situations where they may not be productive and can even be self defeating. By analogy, if we fall in quicksand our tendency would be to struggle. But the more we struggle, the more we need to battle to keep ourselves afloat. However, if we were to use the counter-intuitive action of trying to lie flat and spread one's weight – despite the unpleasant experience of lying back in the wet sand – it would be more productive and considerably safer. Similarly, when faced with an aggressive situation such as a family conflict our habitual tendency may well be to respond in a frightened or angry manner. Either of these responses may aggravate the situation further.

Even so, these examples show the importance of changing patterns of action as a way of tackling problematic situations. Retaining the same patterns of action will tend to allow the situation to continue, complete with its difficulties. Often, it is changes in behaviour that will make the difference. Clearing up after messy family members will allow them to continue making a mess, perhaps in the belief that a benign housework fairy picks up all the clothes and crockery. No matter how disgruntled the housework fairy feels, or how much Prozac she has to eat to keep her on an even keel, the other family members will doubtless far rather endure a bit of bad temper than do any work. In situations like this the solution may lie in adopting a different course of action.

This invites the complex problem of how therapists and clients themselves are to motivate change in people's courses of action. Therefore we will undertake a brief detour into motivation theory in order to identify some lessons for the construction and use of stories in therapeutic contexts.

One of the basic staples of introductory psychology textbooks over the last half century has been Maslow's hierarchy of needs. To remind the reader, let us briefly sketch some of its features. Maslow (1943) defined what he saw to be our general motivational needs. He placed at their base our physiological needs, swiftly followed by safety needs, the need to belong and the need for love, esteem and self actualisation. In general, the motives at the lower end of this hierarchy are activated through deficiency. They become urgent determinants of behaviour when satisfaction is lacking. On the other hand the 'higher' needs such as esteem and self actualisation are seen as 'being needs'.

Of course, Maslow's hierarchy of needs has not withstood the assaults of sceptics and empirically minded researchers very well. It is relatively easy to ridicule, for example, the idea that lower needs must be satisfied before higher needs can be contemplated. Sex is in the base of the hierarchy with the physiological needs, yet very rarely do you hear people saying 'I can't go to work today because I haven't had sex for a week'. Moreover, people can do great creative work under conditions of considerable hardship – an idea that is difficult to reconcile with a strong form of the Maslovian position. Empirical research has neither supported the number of levels in the theory nor the notion that lower levels in the hierarchy must be satisfied before higher level needs will motivate behaviour. Thus, in recent texts, Maslow's theory is covered primarily for its historical interest.

Yet, at the same time, despite these problems, it would be fair to say that this has been one of the most influential 'stories' of the twentieth century. Outside psychology it has been enormously influential in management and organisational theory and educational studies too. As a folktale about human nature it has enjoyed unparalleled success. Moreover, there are important lessons to be learned here about the formulation of successful stories. Maslow's hierarchy puts the Western dream of self improvement – 'from log cabin to president' – on an apparently scientific footing, and gives managers, therapists and educators a way of understanding what they are doing. The story, in other words, does not need to stand up to sceptical scrutiny to be effective. In terms of its enthusiastic adoption it has itself been one of the most influential behaviour change agents – its adoption by textbook writers, therapists, managers and educators is ample testimony to this. Thus we can give form and meaning to our aspirations. Whether it's literally true as an account of how the mind works is just a minor technicality. After 50 years of it soaking into our culture maybe some of it has come true anyway. What is important is the effect on thousands of psychologists and millions of their students, clients and others with whom they come into contact.

Another function that this psychological tale alerts us to is the striving for improvement and perfection that inhabits many of our culturally resonant stories. Classic comedies on UK television through the latter half of the twentieth century saw the likes of Tony Hancock trying to do something worthy perhaps by being a blood donor or an artist. The popular series *Only Fools and Horses* contained stock phrases running through the characters' ill-fated business schemes – 'This time next year Rodney, we'll be millionaires'. It has been said that a good many of these stories betray the British fascination with social class, yet some of the concerns seem to have a broader cross-cultural appeal in the US and Europe.

In presenting stories or anecdotes for behavioural change, it is best to assert the gradual or incremental nature of any change. In other words, change in behaviour takes time and effort. Here we may apply many different metaphors and stories, not least that of a person needing to train properly before running a marathon, or that starving the enemy takes time. In other words, consistent and systematic effort is required. To take the popular example of anxiety disorders, it is often the case that the sessions with the therapist are only the tip of the iceberg in conquering them. Once techniques for inducing relaxation, cognitive restructuring and challenging fears have been introduced it takes a good deal of commitment on the part of the client in between sessions to practise them. There may well be periods of frustration on the part of both therapists and clients at the fact that little progress seems to be made. By way of comparison, consider the example of music. To become a competent musician, capable of performing at grade 8 in the English Board Examinations takes on average 3,000 hours of practice. To be a professional musician takes considerably more, perhaps about 10,000 hours (Howe, 1998). Therefore it is reasonable to expect that other cognitive and motor skills such as the complex and demanding 'skill' of 'not being anxious' or 'not panicking' might be similarly slow to learn. After all, the human body and the human emotional system are considerably more complex than the average musical instrument. Proverbs such as the 'thousand mile journey begins with a single step' come to mind here too.

It is important to emphasise the need to practise new skills and behaviours. For instance, teaching coping skills without providing realistic opportunities to practice is like learning to play tennis from a book! Thus, anything that storytelling can do to consolidate the practice of target behaviour can be helpful in inducing therapeutic change.

The incorporation of apt stories or analogies can help with some of the more onerous aspects of other therapeutic regimes too. For example, in many cognitive behavioural approaches clients are encouraged to keep a diary of desirable or undesirable events to assess frequency and monitor progress. A story that may be applied to help make this aspect of therapy seem suitable to clients is as follows:

ASSISTANT FOR A DAY

A manager is aware that his three shops are losing money and calls together his three assistants for their advice. The first assistant suggests making random changes in the shops without reflecting on their experiences. The second suggests following their collective memory of what is selling well and what is not. The third suggests recording or monitoring what is actually happening in the shops, looking at the figures and patterns and basing decisions on those facts. The manager is not sure which approach is best and finally looks to you for advice. What would you advise him to do?

As can be seen, this story is arranged so that number 3 seems the better option. The key feature of this story is that it draws on existing culturally embedded notions of rationality in solving problems. There's also an implied message that much as problems in business can be solved in this way, problems of the mind can fall under the same rubric. This helps set up the expectation that the technique is part of the cure, and thereby promotes the effectiveness of the therapy. The fact that people can deduce for themselves the rational response also gives them the sense that they have worked it out and thus own part of the process.

In diary keeping by clients to monitor negative automatic thoughts, it may be useful to present the metaphor of an inner bully who gives a negative running commentary to their actions. The client can be encouraged to develop their own inner helper who makes more positive, constructive comments about the client's behaviour. To encourage the dominance of the inner helper you may wish to refer to 'turning up the volume' of its voice and conversely turning down the volume of the inner bully's criticisms. There are legal analogies here too – for example if one is documenting harassment by an unpleasant neighbour or an enraged ex-partner, it is important to document the problems thoroughly as they happen. This strengthens one's case. In the same way, documenting all the anxiety episodes, intrusive thoughts, periods of depression and so on will strengthen one's case in tackling them.

In dealing with anxiety related problems, clients and therapists often have to deal with the rich and varied set of procedures that clients have put in place so that they will not have to face anxiety provoking situations. However, these 'safety behaviours' may prevent their beliefs about the anxiety ever being effectively challenged. A story to illustrate this could proceed as follows:

VANISHING VAMPIRES

The people in a village believe in vampires, and so they become very anxious when it's time to go to sleep at night. In order to keep safe they sleep with cloves of garlic around their necks. A visitor to the village hears about this fear of vampires and asks one of them if anyone in the village had actually seen one. 'Of course not,' he is told. 'No one has seen a vampire so the garlic must be working!' The visitor leaves the village wondering how, then, can the people ever discover that there are no vampires?

This kind of brief story lends itself to a variety of mental health problems, particularly those that involve anxiety, obsessional behaviours and dysfunctional coping strategies. Another example should help consolidate the idea:

DRAGONS KEEP OUT

A man stood on the railway track in a village, waving his arms up and down. On being asked why he was behaving in this manner, he replied that he was keeping the village free from dragons. The villagers informed him that there are no dragons. 'Exactly,' he said and continued waving his arms.

For a client with obsessional behaviours this story may help them to realise that only by not doing something will they gain the opportunity of learning that what they fear will not happen. As with 'vanishing vampires', this brief tale can easily be recalled, confirming for the client that 'there are no dragons' that will appear if they stop the behaviour.

A further use for analogies is in helping clients move towards new goals. It may be valuable to introduce some way of discriminating between behaviours that feel right because they are old, familiar habits, and behaviours that are better because they lead to adaptive change. One useful analogy is old shoes that look a bit tatty and scuffed and leak when it rains. But the owner feels comfortable with them and is reluctant to discard them, not least because he does not want to break in a new pair. This is similar to when we behave in particular ways that we know are unhelpful to us, however we prefer usual, more familiar responses. Also, we anticipate hard work in changing behaviours, just as breaking in new shoes, and might avoid change for this reason. Just as the all too comfortable shoes have provided good service in their time, so too various behaviours may have been useful and even appropriate in the past. For example, a client who chooses not to speak in groups, may have benefited from this reluctance at some time in their life, but the person is compelled to act in ways that are no longer helpful but feel comfortable and familiar to them. Similar responses can occur in patterns of relationships. For example, a client who has been unable to please her mother may then inappropriately seek approval in her other relationships. This approval seeking may have helped the client at one time, say, to avoid excessive criticism as a child, but though familiar it is now unhelpful to her as she is not considering her own needs.

A friend of one of the authors who worked with young offenders recalled using the following story to try to induce some change. While related to the 'shoes' example above this is a little more elaborate and contains more elements. It begins by drawing an analogy between our strategies for getting through life and our outfits. As we gain in experience it is as if we acquire more and more clothes. We have clothes for all the different social events we attend, for going to school, for seeing friends, for visiting grandmothers and so on. For every new event we adapt our outfits somewhat. Eventually, we get weighed down with a suitcase full of clothes and we might decide it is time to sort out the ones we do not need and take them to a charity shop. Moreover, carrying all this excess baggage may mean that we have a great many clothes that are outdated and if we wear them other people will laugh at us. They might have seemed like a good idea at the time but now they may appear very ill-advised. Some kinds of behaviour can be like this too. The sort of thing that got us admired in the school playground might be rather a handicap in the workplace for example. Thus it might be appropriate to leave some aspects of one's behaviour behind as one grows up, as it just gets in the way. There might be things that are more fashionable, suitable or adaptable. The slogan 'dress for success' does not just apply to clothes, but to every other aspect of one's social being. At this point it might be possible to divert the conversation on to some of the more disadvantageous aspects of the client's behaviour. This story, we are told, has been useful in getting through to youngsters who might have an acutely developed sense of what it means to have the right mobile phone, the right trainers or the right casual sportswear.

Metaphors for behaviour can provide a context in which a desired behaviour can be illustrated and, ideally, illustrated repeatedly. The listening client thus has a chance to consider nuances and examples of behaviour at one level, but doesn't ever have to acknowledge a need to learn them. It is simply a story about how someone else performed various aspects of a piece of desirable behaviour and therefore involves no performance pressure for the client.

Metaphor becomes an opportunity for the client to model, think about or consider the 'new' behaviour, and to identify and integrate it in relevant ways. Some therapeutic regimes have emphasised this mental rehearsal, and stories represent one way of enabling this to happen. The use of mental rehearsal techniques has been found effective in sports such as climbing (Jones et al., 2002) and cricketers have noted that it is vital in achieving the 'confidence' they believe is important for successful play (Thelwell & Maynard, 2000). This suggests that the mental rehearsal inherent in telling stories and listening to them might be helpful in the everyday tasks of social life, indeed, in the field of marital and sexual therapy mental rehearsal has been found to be helpful in reactivating desire and gaining confidence in intimate relations (Araoz et al., 2001). Thus, insofar as stories promote this process, they are tapping into a well-established technique for making gains in skilled performance in a variety of areas of human endeavour, not least the sports field and the bedroom.

An analogy that promotes externalising is the notion of 'starving the enemy'. Here we are thinking about overcoming an enemy (and hence a problem) through the process of starvation. This analogy can help to emphasise the importance for clients in using a consistent and sustained approach to tackling their difficulties. It may serve as a model for people with obsessive disorders who need to adopt a total programme of starving the enemy. For an 'enemy' to be starved, it requires complete absence of food. Giving in from time to time will prolong the situation. In dealing with obsessional behaviour, setbacks caused by occasionally performing the compulsions will undermine progress and maintain disorder.

Yet another analogy that can be used to emphasise that facing up to our fears is the only truly effective way to overcome them is the scenario of standing up to the school bully. With the school bully, for example, you know if you give in to the bully on one occasion by, say, handing over pocket money or doing their homework for them, the bully is likely to repeat their requests. While giving over pocket money may seem the easier solution in the short term, in the long term it is more likely to create further problems and distress. Avoiding the bully, just as we might avoid what we fear, whether this be our phobias or the consequences of not performing a compulsive behaviour, might bring short-term relief but will not deal with the problem for the long term.

A similar analogy can be built around the notion of toddler tantrums and needing a firm and consistent approach. Just like a toddler might demand sweets at a supermarket checkout, you know if you give into them you increase the likelihood that this demand will become a fixed ritual every time you go to the shops. However, you also know that a refusal can escalate a tantrum and be uncomfortable and embarrassing to deal with there and then. Yet holding firm on your decision and dealing with the fallout will be worth it in the long term. Just like facing our fears can lead to a distressing increase in our anxiety, holding in there and not giving ourselves over to the fear will bring benefits in time.

We know from chapter 1 that the folktales detailed by Propp tend to emphasise the transformation of states of affairs or persons through action. There are, as well as pre-revolutionary Russian folktales, of course many more popular examples from the twentieth century. For example, in this popular context, Umberto Eco (1966) attempted to identify the essential features of a James Bond story. Again, the emphasis of stories on the action of the protagonists to change circumstances and indeed the world are apparent in the narrative features Eco identifies. Ian Fleming's original novels and the subsequent films tend to have, for example, the following features:

> *M moves and gives a task to Bond.*
> *The villain moves and appears to Bond.*
> *Bond moves and gives a first 'check' (by analogy with chess, Bond makes a challenging move) to the villain or the villain gives first check to Bond.*
> *Woman moves and shows herself to Bond.*
> *Bond consumes woman: possesses her or begins her seduction.*
> *The villain captures Bond.*
> *The villain tortures Bond.*
> *Bond conquers the villain.*
> *Bond convalescing enjoys woman, whom he then loses.*
>
> (Eco, 1966, p. 52)

This sequence of actions is again subdivided into further motifs or set pieces in the films. The villain is often of superior strength and may command superior firepower yet Bond supervenes through a combination of luck, strategy and cunning. There are messages here for many everyday situations. This kind of story structure is similar to that of tales of standing up to the school bully or remaining firm in the face of toddler tantrums, and can be metaphors for learning to face fears, and tolerate certain amounts of anxiety, in order to eventually overcome them. These kinds of stories of heroes tackling villains also include the idea that avoidance just stores up problems for the future in that if an individual gives in they will always have to give in. Moreover, it need not be James Bond. It is possible to identify similar features in accounts of David and Goliath or Batman movies. Generally, the adversary is a worthy one and vanquishing him represents a significant victory. These story metaphors do something else too – that is, the problem is personified and externalised. This is often seen as a valuable technique. It has been promoted most extensively by Michael White, who is well known for his contributions to family and narrative therapies. As reported by Tomm (1989), the idea of externalising began when White made a significant discovery. He was working with children who had not mastered bowel control (encophresis) at the usual age, and he invented the phrase 'Sneaky Poo' to describe the problem when he talked to the children about it. Thus by personifying the problem he 'externalised it' so that it could be talked about as an entity separate from the child. In the therapeutic dialogue, White might ask the child questions like: 'Have you ever had Sneaky Poo sneak up on you and pop into your pants when you were busy playing?' and 'Have you ever beaten Sneaky Poo?'. By this manoeuvre the problem is thought of as 'Sneaky Poo's' and not the child's and this means that the parents have less reason to criticise and blame the child or to blame themselves. Instead this approach opens a space to explore new efforts in problem solving. Since everyone is fighting the same 'troublemaker' and family members are no longer at loggerheads, it is easier for the child and parents to 'join forces in beating Sneaky Poo'. As a result, the therapeutic process is facilitated.

But there is still more to the process of externalising with the use of an apt story or metaphor. Once a problem has been externalised the client can be invited to escape the oppression of the labelling, as for example an encophretic child, or in some of White's work, a person with 'schizophrenia'. Thus they can set their lives in the direction that they prefer. Clients are asked questions like: 'How ready are you to take a further step against the voice of anorexia?'. In this way, new strategies to combat anorexia are envisioned in therapy and the client is empowered rather than being left feeling helpless. As with storytelling, this kind of approach revolves around the apt metaphor and no pressure is brought to bear on clients to take a particular course of action. Again like storytelling, White's approach emphasises the alternatives that might be available to clients. This process of externalising can be quite liberating for clients who may have spent many years entrapped in their difficulties.

These metaphors are not quite the same as a more extended story or folktale, yet they can be used as a device to crack the problem open and facilitate new ways of talking about it. For example, take the case of a woman particularly concerned about the cleanliness of her windows. She cleaned them almost every day. It was very difficult for her to desist from this behaviour, and when she was not actually cleaning them she was checking them for marks. In discussing the increasing amount of time this was taking up and how it was interfering with her working life, we might come up with a useful notion akin to that of 'Sneaky Poo' – the 'Phantom Fingermarker' whose telltale prints could be discovered on the freshly polished glass, and on other surfaces such as doors and walls. Not succumbing to these repetitive compulsions is, in a sense, to do with not giving in to her adversary the 'Phantom Fingermarker', whose objective was to waste as much of her time as possible.

This process of developing stories or metaphors may well work most effectively if it is pursued flexibly. As Dwivedi (1997) argues, we need to cultivate different responses for different contexts. For example, when we have healthy legs, jogging can be very useful as it helps to keep the legs healthy. On the other hand, applying a plaster cast can be an unhealthy thing to do to a healthy leg, but it can be very helpful when applied to a broken leg, for which jogging would be damaging.

In the same way it could be argued that semi-fictional characters such as Sneaky Poo or the Phantom Fingermarker might be rather problematic in clients who were already paranoid or delusional. However, their judicious use with clients who could see the humour and the fictionality of these devices may well just give the insight needed to precipitate effective change.

In addition to the change processes outlined above that take both time and consistency, many difficulties that face clients can seem overwhelming because of their complexity. This experience of being overwhelmed can mean that the client focuses on everything that needs to be done rather than attempting to change any aspect of their difficulties. In these circumstances it would be helpful to instil the notion of 'chunking down' difficulties into smaller, more manageable units that can be addressed in turn. This realistic and achievable approach to change can be introduced and demonstrated with the help of stories. For example, to illustrate the unhelpful tendency to dwell unproductively on tasks, we might talk about a marathon runner. Imagine at the start line, if the runner was to dwell on the total distance he had to run, all those individual steps, the pain that would be involved, the blisters, the heat and other difficulties. We might expect that he would feel like giving up. It would benefit the runner not to magnify the task until it becomes impossible to do anything. A better approach would be to 'chunk down' the total task into smaller pieces, such as focusing on getting through one mile.

Further, if someone was starting to train to run a marathon it would be unreasonable to expect them to be able to do the 26 miles straight off. It becomes more manageable if smaller targets are set and the training is regular. Similarly beating an anxiety disorder takes stamina, and this can be built up and practised regularly. Physical exercise is most effective when practised three times a week or more, so the same can be argued to be true of psychological interventions. Many people subscribe to gyms, health clubs and aerobic classes, start with a rush of enthusiasm and then their attendance peters out after a few weeks. That way little is achieved and only the gym proprietors benefit. Practising the skills and strategies regularly, in a sense enables you to 'get your money's' worth out of the technique.

Using a 'digging in sand' metaphor can be quite useful when preparing clients to begin to tackle their difficulties. When digging in dry sand the sand runs down to fill the hole almost as fast as you can dig. By analogy, attempting to change behaviour is not always as simple, straightforward or uncomplicated as we would wish. It can be a messy process with various issues and subsequent difficulties (like the sides falling in) as the client begins to tackle one problem behaviour. Thus, in anxiety disorders, one set of symptoms may be reduced but others may spring up or intensify and the problem shifts. It takes a certain amount of dedicated labour to continue the process despite such setbacks and distractions. After the initial difficulties it gets easier.

Lakoff (1987) notes, in *Women, fire and dangerous things*, that anger has often been associated with the sense of things getting hot, boiling and pressure building up. Thus, we have opposing ideas about cooling off and releasing pressure. At a metaphorical level we can present the idea of carrying a stress bottle around with us. This bottle fills over a lifetime with a variety of experiences and stresses. Eventually it becomes so full that if even one more trivial thing happens, the cork flies out of the bottle in an explosion of anger. Using this metaphor with the client, it is then possible to discuss ways of learning to empty the bottle so they have more of a threshold for further daily stresses. Ways of reducing the bottled up stress include relaxation, humour, talking to others, exercise, using assertiveness rather than simply fuming ineffectively and so on.

A helpful analogy for making sense of anxieties and other emotions in everyday life is to think about traffic lights at a busy road junction. The general conformity of motorists is to go only when the light is green and to stop when the light is red. The question that arises from observing this routine behaviour is this: why do drivers obey the lights? The goal of the traffic light analogy is to propose to listeners that conforming behaviour does not result from fear of punishment – there is not a police officer at every intersection, and accidents are relatively rare in relation to the volume of traffic. Rather, observance of the law is the product of the shared desire of self interested motorists to get through the intersection safely and to proceed to their destinations. If no one obeyed the directions implied by the colours of the lights, there would be numerous collisions. The motorists' prospects for arriving safely at their destinations would be greatly endangered if not entirely defeated. This social choreography is usually achieved without any great fear or anxiety on behalf of the motorists. Usually, if the lights are red for us, we stop, without necessarily thinking 'if I don't stop I'll crash into other drivers and die'. Only when our brakes fail do we get in touch with our fears. Usually we might stop well before the point of anxiety is reached. This particular idea is versatile and again can be used for any kind of problem that involves anxiety and the defences that the person uses to avoid it, from obsessive compulsive rituals to avoiding going out. For example, a man whom one of the authors knew became increasingly restricted by his fear that if he went into a crowded place such as a town centre or a pub, a fight would break out and he would become involved. By analogy with traffic lights, among other things, it was gradually possible to convince him that most behaviour in public places was fairly careful, courteous and rule governed, and it was possible to withstand most minor infractions without coming to blows. He disclosed that he had once seen a man badly injured with a beer bottle in a fracas in a pub and this fear had nagged him ever since. Thinking about the people in crowded places as having brake lights and indicators too was helpful as it was amusing. Thus the analogy was elaborated on over time as it became more convincing to think of relations in public in terms of road traffic.

Another example is the 'Expensive insurance policy'. For example, one might start by asking 'Is your house insured?' and 'Are you protected for fire? Burglaries? Accidents?' And so on. The list can become increasingly absurd and unlikely. 'Are you insured for acts of war? Invasion by Martians? What if I said I could provide you with a policy, which covered you for every eventuality for a mere 3 million pounds. Would you buy it?' Most clients say no to this. Then a parallel can be drawn with their obsessions, in that these are ensuring safety at enormous cost to their own life.

The process of externalisation is promoted further for anxiety disorders by Phillipson (2002), who suggests that even in clients without any religious convictions, conceptualising the disorder as a demon, separate from one's own identity, seems to be an apt choice. The game plan of both a demon and the anxiety disorder as a whole are conceptualised by Phillipson as follows:

1. To seduce a person into doing its bidding by promising relief just around the corner. Often the obsessive compulsive demon will convince the victim that only one more reassurance will resolve the dilemma and provide more than momentary relief.
2. To exploit moments of weakness and materialise at the worst possible times in a person's life (e.g. when it is perceived as absolutely disastrous to become anxious).
3. To choke the victim more each time he struggles to get away.

Thus by making the game plan explicit, the client is provided with a way of anticipating the likely manoeuvres of the disorder and guides for action to counteract it. The game plan of this anxiety disorder also closely resembles that of the neighbourhood bully, which clients might be able to remember from their childhoods. As children, we are told that if we muster up the courage to actually challenge the bully and call his or her bluff, the aggressor will back down. Unfortunately, in real life this might prove quite a struggle and even, on occasions, fail. However, with the demons of obsessive compulsive disorder, this may be easier. In our clinical experience, those clients who have genuinely challenged the demon to do its worst, and are perfectly willing to confront and endure tremendous discomfort, even death itself, have made the most dramatic progress. They, in fact, have experienced the least amount of pain while performing exposure exercises. This exemplifies the critical nature of understanding the mental paradox. The more pain one is willing to endure, the less it is experienced.

It is also often the case that many attempts must be made before the right 'design' for one's resistance to fears is achieved. Often, success is only possible after many futile attempts. By way of example here, Freeman Dyson, the physicist, writer and futurologist has this to say about bicycles: 'You can't possibly get a good technology going without an enormous number of failures. It's a universal rule. If you look at bicycles, there were thousands of weird models built and tried before they found the one that really worked. You could never design a bicycle theoretically. Even now, after we've been building them for 100 years, it's very difficult to understand just why a bicycle works – it's even difficult to formulate it as a mathematical problem. But just by trial and error, we found out how to do it, and the error was essential. The same is true of airplanes' (Dyson, interviewed by Brand, 1998). This then highlights the importance of being flexible about adapting design solutions, whether in engineering or in behaviour. The same kind of story could be told of sewing machines, where many attempts were made to develop a viable one, and inventors and entrepreneurs suffered attacks by marauding tailors, jealously protecting their trade. In this case some of the most important innovations to facilitate machine sewing, such as the eye in the tip of the needle, are believed to have come from dreams – Elias Howe reported that he had dreamed of men with spears attacking him. The spears each had a curious oval hole near the point. This, then, led to the design of sewing machine needles as we now know them. Inspiration for our strategies to defeat anxieties or depressive moods, then, can come from many quarters.

A useful story illuminating the consequence of not adapting is Dr Seuss's 'The Zax', which is a tale about two fantastic characters, one who always heads north and one who is always determined on going south. When they bump into one another, a squabble breaks out:

'Look here, now!' the North-Going Zax said. 'I say! You are blocking my path. You are right in my way. I'm a North-Going Zax and I always go north. Get out of my way, now, and let me go forth!'

Of course the South-Going Zax is just as proud and angry, and refuses to budge, arguing that: 'I'll stay here, not budging! I can and I will. If it makes you and me and the whole world stand still!'

The consequences, while humorous, are very telling:

'Well … Of course the world didn't *stand still. The world grew. In a couple of years, the new highway came through. And they built it right over those two stubborn Zax. And left them there, standing un-budged in their tracks.'*

(Adapted from Seuss, 1998, pp. 26–35).

Thus, people who respond in inflexible ways can be gently encouraged to change their responses both in terms of emotions and also behaviour. This story could be used to illustrate the importance of flexibility for success. The more choices of action you have the more chance of success. Clients can be encouraged to keep evaluating and changing what they do until they get what they want. This may seem obvious, but often it is important to challenge well-developed yet unhelpful ways of doing something. This may happen for example in relationships where couples constantly have the same argument.

So far we have mentioned a number of ideas and strategies for assisting in dealing with anxieties and fears. These, in a sense, are the jewel in the crown of therapeutic practice. A great many therapists cut their clinical teeth on the cluster of problems that are now called anxiety disorders, from psychoanalysis to cognitive behavioural therapy. It is now appropriate to consider once more the issue of changing behaviour itself.

A good deal of what has been attempted in the form of behaviour change relates to health education, particularly with regard to drugs, sex or safety precautions of various kinds, such as wearing helmets, seatbelts or using machinery guards. Therefore, it is worth looking at some of this research and theory if we are concerned with changing behaviour. With some issues in clinical settings it is the behaviour change that is central and the attitude change is more peripheral, especially when we are dealing with behaviour changes that dramatically reduce the risks to which clients are subject.

The traditional approach to teaching children safety in workshops and laboratories at school often involves the teacher responsible for the 'safety talk' telling tales of the severe consequences of not complying with the safety precautions. Accounts of acid burns, hands being ripped off in lathes and welding gas bottles exploding were a basic staple of these talks. Of course, on closer reflection, the stories of catastrophic consequences, which had usually befallen some unspecified child in another class or another year group, appeared less than credible. Surely if this had happened there would have been an investigation by the police or civil authorities, and even disciplinary action or prosecution against the teacher concerned. These tragic events would very likely not form part of a macabre story to terrify the next year group, especially as some of the people involved would still be in the school. Nevertheless, a competent teacher could keep a class of fidgety 12 year olds transfixed with this kind of story.

This, then, was the stuff that our teachers, never formally schooled in the art of storytelling therapy or narratives as a tool of behaviour change, had hit upon as a way of bringing an otherwise boring safety talk to life.

This illustrates one of the basic functions of storytelling in the hope of inducing some sort of behaviour change. It performs the basic functions of alerting someone to the hazards, making them appear to apply to the audience in question – using the example of an unfortunate child who met a sticky end – and advising the audience of how to avoid the same fate. In psychology, a good deal of the research that has attempted to look at this process has been concerned with getting people to change to more healthy behaviours – eating less fat, taking more exercise, wearing more condoms and taking their medication as directed. Much of the literature has conceptualised this process in terms of cognitive, attitudinal, psychosocial and demographic variables. The widely known 'health belief model' is generally used to make sense of attitudinal and behavioural change towards more desirable patterns of conduct. Different authors have formulated the idea in slightly different ways, but broadly the model suggests that the likelihood that an individual will take action concerning a health or safety issue is determined by the person seeing the problem as being relevant to themselves in the first place, their desire to take action and by the perceived benefits of the action weighed against the perceived costs of taking such action. Researchers using this kind of approach have looked at how an individual estimates their susceptibility to a problem and the benefits of detection and treatment for that particular illness (Becker, 1974; Hochbaum et al., 1992). The individual's health behaviour in this formulation will be based on their perception of how susceptible they are to the hazard or illness in question, and by their expectation of benefits, adverse experiences and barriers they are likely to encounter as a result of the recommended action.

Whereas this is somewhat different from the processes of psychotherapy, we can see some parallels too. Individuals undertaking therapy have to see a particular formulation of their difficulties as being relevant to them, and have to appreciate that the therapeutically desirable course of action will be worthwhile – that its benefits will outweigh the costs. An example might be that the hard work involved in tackling anxiety by learning relaxation techniques, challenging unhelpful thoughts and tackling fears will ultimately be beneficial.

Our concern here is that adopting a therapeutic model that sees people as these kinds of rational beings who undertake their homework exercises between appointments because they genuinely want to get better will be pretty frustrating for the therapist and ultimately the client, because often this is not what people do.

Indeed, such is the vigour with which these attitudinal and cognitive conceptions of the compliance process are pursued that some theorists talk of 'the disease of non-adherence' and the need for practitioners to 'diagnose' and commence 'therapy' for the condition (Chisholm, 2002, p. 31). This enthusiasm for conceptualising the issue in terms of the cognitive and attitudinal features of health belief models is justified in terms of the relative success of these models in health promotion initiatives. Yet a number of notes of caution need to be sounded.

First, and most importantly, from our point of view, it is not focused on therapeutic encounters themselves. There is a lot to be accomplished in getting clients to see their problem in terms that therapy can tackle and suggesting the appropriate changes in behaviour at health encounters themselves. The kinds of data on which a good deal of research on outcomes or compliance with recommendations is based, are derived from questionnaire and standard interviews, and are very rarely based on the rough and tumble of therapeutic interactions. It is based in a kind of philosophical nominalism, which presupposes that attitudes and beliefs pre-exist individuals' behaviour after therapy. It may equally be, as we have discussed above, that the action itself helps to create the attitude. Or, equally, that revised patterns of action help place the client in new social settings, which help revise their attitudes. In either event, the role stories could have is crucial as they provide a means of placing the client – either in imagination or in practice – in these new settings.

The individualistic focus of health belief models is a source of further difficulty. We cannot easily see the practitioners or patients in this system as being part of broader linguistic, storytelling or sense making communities or frameworks of understanding. Certainly, social support networks and the like are sometimes included as variables in the model (Chisholm, 2002). Yet these are not accorded a constitutive role in giving shape and form to the therapeutic process, nor as helping to give form to the symptoms of the complaint. When clients, friends and acquaintances tell us for example that they thought they were alone until they saw their problem featured on a daytime talk show or a soap opera, this illustrates the importance of stories as a way of giving form to one's malaise and suggesting a course of action. The stories that others tell and which are circulated in the mass media are deployed with great alacrity in making sense of one's problems. Illnesses and distress are also understood, of course, in terms of stories from the client's own family.

The cheerful optimism of much existing writing on psychotherapeutic processes from a cognitive behavioural perspective sheds little light on why some therapeutic change processes flourish and grow and are widely admired, and then suddenly collapse like a burst balloon, or why some people endure the most severe tribulations and difficulties, while others stumble at the first setback. The rather mechanistic analysis of emotion, cognition and behaviour that tends to be applied to these problems has not always been much help to us. In particular it doesn't fit the complexity, the mess, the chaos, the confusion, the living core of people in their everyday social contexts. Moreover, it is not necessarily successful in persuading people to change. That is why stories, precisely because they can be nuanced, lifelike and filled with the quotidian mess of everyday life may enable clients and professionals to make more headway. Rather than exhorting change in dysfunctional cognitions, stories show how thoughts and actions may be dysfunctional, advantageous or somewhere in between. In particular, the advantage of stories in these circumstances is that they invite the listener to make some headway themselves as they imagine themselves changing their lives. This, then, may well be more effective in the longer term because the listener feels that any changes are a good idea. This may work better than overt encouragement from therapists.

To facilitate this, exploiting the power of stories to help implement behaviour change can sometimes involve using them to get the audience to imagine what would happen if we got the benefits of success, happiness, love and so on in an interesting, rapid and exciting way. What kinds of people could we become! As Denning (2000) argues, by stimulating the listeners to think actively about the implications, they can get a feel for what it will be like to do things differently.

Denning (2000) calls these kind of stories that allow the listeners' minds to race ahead and imagine the implications of using and elaborating the same idea in other contexts with which the listeners are familiar, 'springboard stories'. Thus, through extrapolating the narrative, the seeds of change can be planted in the listeners' minds, not as a vague, abstract, inert idea, but as Denning calls it 'an idea that is pulsing, kicking, breathing, exciting and alive'.

Often therapeutic changes that need to be implemented to tackle real world problems in complex social networks are themselves complex, and have many dimensions and facets. Not all of them can be fully understood when therapists and clients embark on the change process. Resistance may well appear when a bold new change idea emerges. The difficulty for participants in the therapeutic process in such situations is how to turn resistance into enthusiasm when they only partially understand the idea. Often an attempt to explain in detail the theory behind therapeutic processes can kill enthusiasm before therapy is implemented. Also, when working with anxious clients, memory and concentration for such detail may be compromised. The advantage of storytelling in these circumstances is that it affords a less imposing means by which the listener can receive information by filling in the blanks for themselves as the change process proceeds.

The stories that were successful for Denning (2000) in his work on organisational change – which in some ways is similar to therapeutic change – had certain characteristics. These stories were told from the perspective of a single protagonist in a predicament that was somehow prototypical – it had many of the key elements of the current dilemma, matter in hand or social setting. The themes of the explicit story were familiar to that particular audience, and represented the same sort of predicament that the proposed changes were meant to solve. The successful stories also had an element of strangeness or incongruity for the listeners, in such a way as to command their attention and stimulate their imaginations. Yet, at the same time as being incongruous, the stories were plausible and familiar, as Denning describes it 'almost like a premonition' of what the future could be like. Denning also recommends trying to make the story embody the change proposal as much as possible, using real examples, and using extrapolations into the future to complete the picture. Despite all this forethought and planning that goes into stories, they work best, says Denning, if they are told as simply and as briefly as possible. Speed and conciseness are important, he says, because as an instigator of change he was less interested in conveying exact details of what happens in the explicit story than he was in sparking new stories in the hearers' minds, which they would reinvent and invest with the context of their own environments. We would support this point. That is, the stories need to have inviting spaces in them in which people can imagine themselves. For the same reason, Denning's stories all had happy endings so as to make it easy for the listeners to make the imaginative leap from the explicit story that is overtly told, to the implicit story that is elicited in listeners' minds.

Storytelling is not a panacea for facilitating change in people's behaviour. It is only as good as the idea being conveyed or the strategy being advocated. That, in itself, is in the hands of our imagination and the structural constraints within which therapists and clients have to work. If the story is a poor one, and does not suit the context, storytelling may well disclose its inadequacy. But even when the underlying idea is good, there are times when storytelling is ineffective. On some occasions it may well be that a story or anecdote will not enable the listener to grasp the concept. Experienced storytellers in business contexts have noted that sometimes clients might listen to the story and ask more questions about the details of the event described. This is taken as an indication that people have not fully grasped the 'take home message'. It suggests that people are getting concerned with the details of the explicit story, which might be interesting, but that the performance has failed to elicit the implicit story. The implicit story is the one which in Denning's formulation springs the listener to a new level of understanding of the possibilities of change being envisaged.

REFERENCES

Ajzen, I. (2000) Nature and operation of attitudes. *Annual Review of Psychology*, **52**, 27–58.

Araoz, D., Burte, J. & Goldin, E. (2001) Sexual hypnotherapy for couples and family counselors. *Family Journal: Counselling and Therapy for Couples and Families*, 9(1), 75–81.

Becker, M. H. (1974) The Health Belief Model and personal health behaviour. *Health Education Monographs*, **2** (whole part 4).

Brand, S. (1998) Freeman Dyson's brain, *Wired* online magazine. http://www.wired.com/wired/archive/6.02/dyson.html.

Brehm, J. (1956) Post-decision changes in the desirability of alternatives. *Journal of Abnormal and Social Psychology*, **52**, 384–9.

Chisholm, M. (2002) Enhancing transplant patients' adherence to medication therapy. *Clinical Transplantation*, **16**, 30–8.

Denning, S. (2000) *The springboard: How storytelling ignites action in knowledge organisations.* Boston: Butterworth Heinemann.

Dwivedi, K. N. (Ed.)(1997) *The therapeutic use of stories.* London: Routledge.

Eco, U. (1966) Narrative structure in Fleming. In E. del Buono & U. Eco (Eds.). *The Bond affair.* London: Macdonald.

Festinger, L. & Carlsmith, J. M. (1959) Cognitive consequences of forced compliance. *Journal of Abnormal and Social Psychology*, **58**, 203–10.

Harris, T., Brown, G. W. & Robinson, R. (1999) Befriending as an intervention for chronic depression among women in an inner city. *British Journal of Psychiatry*, **174**, 219–24.

Hobden, K. L. & Olson, J. M. (1994) From jest to antipathy: Disparagement humour as a source of dissonance motivated attitude change. *Basic and Applied Social Psychology*, **15**, 239–49.

Hochbaum, G. M., Sorenson, J. R., & Lorig, K. (1992). Theory in Health Education Practice. *Health Education Quarterly*, **19**(3), 293–313.

Howe, M. J. A. (1998) *IQ in question: The truth about intelligence.* London: Sage Publications.

James, W. (1890, reprinted 1950) *The principles of psychology*, volume 2. New York: Dover Publications.

Jones, M. V., Mace, R. D., Bray, S. R., MacRae, A. W. & Stockbridge, C. (2002) The impact of motivational imagery on the emotional state and self-efficacy levels of novice climbers. *Journal of Sport Behaviour,* **25**(1), 57–73.

Keijsers, G. P. J. (1999) Preliminary results of a new instrument to assess patient motivation for treatment in cognitive-behaviour therapy. *Behavioural and Cognitive Psychotherapy*, **27**(2), 165–79.

Knox, R. E. & Inkster, J. A. (1968) Post decision dissonance at post time. *Journal of Personality and Social Psychology*, **8**, 319–23.

Lakoff, G. (1987) *Women, fire and dangerous things: What categories reveal about the mind.* Chicago: University of Chicago Press.

Leippe, M. R. & Eisenstadt, D. (1994) Generalisation of dissonance reduction: Decreasing prejudice through reduced compliance. *Journal of Personality and Social Psychology*, **67**, 395–413.

Maslow, A. H. (1943) A theory of human motivation. *Psychological Review*, **50**, 370–96.

Phillipson. S. (2002) Speak of the devil. http://www.ocdonline.com/articlephillipson3.htm.

Rutter, D. & Quine, L. (2002) *Changing health behaviour: Intervention and research with social cognition models.* Buckingham: Open University Press.

Schlenker, B. R., Dlugoleki, D. W. & Doherty, K. (1994) The impact of self presentations on self appraisals and behaviour: the power of public commitment. *Personality and Social Psychology Bulletin*, **20**, 20–33.

Seuss, Dr (1998) *The Sneetches and other stories.* London: Collins.

Teri, L. & Lewinsohn, P. (1986) Individual and group treatment of unipolar depression: Comparison of treatment outcome and predictors of successful treatment outcome. *Behaviour Therapy*, **17**(3), 215–28.

Thelwell, R. C. & Maynard, I. W. (2000) Professional cricketers' perceptions of the importance of antecedents influencing repeatable good performance. *Perceptual and Motor Skills*, **90**(2), 649–58.

Tice, D. M. (1992) Self concept change and self presentation: The looking glass self is also a magnifying glass. *Journal of Personality and Social Psychology*, **63**, 435–51.

Tomm, K. (1989) Externalizing the problem and internalizing personal agency. *Journal of Strategic and Systemic Therapies*, **8**(1), 54–9.

Younger, J. C., Walker, L. & Arrowood, J. A.(1977) Post-decision dissonance at the fair. *Personality and Social Psychology Bulletin*, **3**, 284–7.

5 SELF IMAGE, DEVELOPMENT AND NURTURE

This chapter examines how therapists can use stories to change clients' self image. We will elaborate on what we mean by self image in more detail later, but for the moment let us consider a few of the many elements, which might go to make it up. A self image might comprise a person's social image in different social contexts, their body image, their values, their work roles, their gender identities and their efforts at impression management. Amidst this diversity, most people nevertheless have some sort of sense of who they are. Moreover, in many therapeutic traditions a strong self image is believed to be desirable. Indeed, people's attitudes to themselves, in the form of self esteem, locus of control and a sense of self efficacy are at the heart of many therapeutic activities. It is often assumed that the self is something we can work on and enhance, by means of self help, self nurturing or self improvement. Thus, the more we look after our 'selves' the better our self esteem and confidence. By nurturing our 'selves', it is believed, we are less likely to succumb to anxiety, depression or remain in unfulfilling relationships.

In Western culture there is a long tradition of this kind of self care. As the historian and philosopher Michel Foucault notes, an ethic of self care (Foucault, 1986) has existed since the ancient Greeks. Therapists and clients who actively participate in reflective storytelling, journal keeping and self analysis are partaking in the ancient notion of the 'cultivation of the self', a potentially lifelong process of gaining self knowledge. Foucault describes how this ethic of self care was popularised in the ancient Greek culture. Writers such as Seneca, the dramatist and poet, and Epictetus, the slave turned philosopher, described how people needed to devote themselves to this practice. Foucault explains how Plato and his followers viewed the ethic of self care as a dialectical structure, which involved an interplay between speaking, listening and writing. By the time of the Stoics, the care of the self became an internalised habit, where one internally reflected for a sense of truth. The practitioner would silently listen to a lecture or read a text and contemplate it, perhaps write about it. The Stoics' notions of self care and self discovery also included the practice of *askesis*, or self discipline obtained through the acquisition of truth (Foucault, 1997, p. 238). Through a kind of storytelling dialogue with oneself and others, one made corrections and searched for a greater sense of self truth so that one might lead a fuller life. This kind of self care and self nurturing was believed to be a kind of duty for citizens and extended beyond their daily chores and into their personal lives. This can be seen in the explosion of personal writing in later classical civilisation. Writing about oneself became a 'true social practice' (Foucault, 1986, p. 51). Reflective manuscripts were a popular method for people to participate in acts of self cultivation. It did not have the punitive or penitential function, as it did in later Christian notions of confession, but was entirely prescriptive. People wrote reflectively and studied these reflections 'in order to reactivate its principles and ensure their correct application in the future' (Foucault, 1986, p. 61). Once literate citizens began to feel it was important to be able to tell the story of themselves, this opened up a number of possibilities for both consciousness and social connection. This kind of writing about the self in notebooks (*hypmnemata*) served as a kind of 'administrative review' where people would look back at their daily actions, beliefs and conversations to make continual improvements in their personae just as a governmental body might record events or changes in society and law (Foucault, 1997). The *hypomnemata* linked one's personal writing to the care of the self, and turned this reflective writing about the self into a social practice. A person's reflections were more than just a means for personal improvement. Writing was a means towards possible social change too.

The *hypomnemata* were also a kind of personal collection of the stories of other people and served a complex role in one's personal growth. The ancient Greeks used these notebooks to reflect on 'quotations, fragments of works, examples and actions to which one had been witness of or of which one had read the account, reflections or reasonings which one had heard or which had come to mind' (Foucault, 1997, p. 246). These notebooks sometimes served as spring-boards for larger, more complex writings. This process involved a kind of constant development of the self as one reflected on one's own personal collection of stories, which was a key factor in the ethic of self care. One would subsequently re-read these writings and meditate on their meanings so as to constantly monitor and assimilate whatever new learning had occurred. In classical civilisations philosophy itself was conceived as a practice of self regulation through a continuous project of self representation. Such a project means becoming concerned with relationships of truth, power and desire through the anecdotes. The practice of liberty is closely allied to the 'care of the self' in this context, and it is believed to prevent oppression and promote the striving for authenticity, as well as solidarity and plurality in our lives as individuals and communities.

Thus, following on from these ancient ideas – which are themselves transmitted through stories – we are more likely to change our attitudes and behaviours in a positive way if we assimilate more self nurturing and liberatory stories. In other words, we might grow less self critical or self damning. Thus in this chapter we explore a range of stories that illustrate the importance of this kind of 'care of the self' and show how they might be used to give clients the opportunity to choose pathways that will strengthen their 'sense of self' in a positive and affirmative way.

For example, there is a good deal of interest in the concept of self criticism (Kurman et al., 2003) as a mediating factor in depression and low self esteem. This is especially the case if the self criticism is emotional rather than constructive. If people are self critical this can be seen as 'coaching' themselves in a negative way, bringing themselves a few rungs down the ladder at every turn. Often, in such cases the person will attack himself or herself as being stupid, or too slow, or simply useless. One way of encouraging a more positive self image can be by telling the story (adapted from Otto, 2000) of a young professional playing a sport (tailoring the choice to the client's gender and background) in which he or she makes a costly mistake. The mistake is heavily criticised by the young person's coach – Coach A. This 'emotional' criticism makes the young player more nervous than ever and he or she makes even more mistakes. At this point, Coach B approaches the player and acknowledges that he or she had made an error, but gives the player useful tips on how to improve their play, in other words, 'constructive self criticism'. While still disappointed in the failure, this advice results in fewer mistakes being made and enables the player to develop in confidence. Following this story, you can get your client to reflect on how they 'coach' or 'manage' themselves. When they 'hear' Coach A, they should be encouraged to 'bring on' Coach B. Thus, encouraging clients to reflect on how they are 'coaching' themselves, may yield a different and more constructive kind of coaching.

In order to defuse some of the self criticism it might be worthwhile to tackle also the sense of difference or failure on which it might be founded. Hans Christian Anderson's classic children's tale of *The Ugly Duckling* can teach us that it's OK to be different and not immediately accepted or recognised by everyone else. Barker (1996) endorses the Ugly Duckling too, in suggesting possible stories to use with clients who present with feelings such as 'It's hopeless. I'll never make it'. This story shows how, despairing and isolated, we later can go through a period of transition and discover that we are more than – and different from – what we originally thought.

A similar tale can be found in the classic Disney film – now more than 60 years old – of Dumbo the elephant. The themes in this film include tolerance of differences and the importance of believing in yourself. The other elephants laughed at Dumbo when he arrived at the circus because of his excessively big ears. Yet he surpassed them all when he learned to fly. The film also provides an opportunity to demonstrate empathy by asking listeners how they would feel if everyone laughed at them the way the animals laugh at Dumbo, and how important it is to Dumbo to have a friend like Timothy the mouse. Timothy represents a more helpful, supportive voice on the shoulder of Dumbo. Clients may be encouraged to learn to be their own Timothy mouse.

Likewise, the theme of persistence at an apparently hopeless task can be illustrated by the tale of the 'discovery' of the Americas. In Christopher Columbus's journal of his epic voyage to discover a new passage to the Indies he records that the crew remonstrated and complained about the length of the voyage. Some accounts embroider these grievances into a 'mutiny'. Yet, a few nights later, a light was seen ahead of the ships and the following morning a sailor named Rodrigo de Triana on 'The Pinta' is credited with being the first to spot the land itself. This, then, highlights the importance of pressing on despite doubts and the efforts of one's more faint-hearted compatriots to turn back. Indeed, the Columbus story itself is interesting as it highlights the struggle Columbus himself had to raise support for his voyage from the great mercantile nations of Europe.

Despite the achievement Columbus was a little misguided by the standards of contemporary geography. Had the Americas not been in the way, he would probably have arrived quite near the mouth of the Yang-tse-Kiang River, in China, which was what he was seeking. For nearly a generation afterwards he and his followers supposed that the coast of that region was what they had found. Achievements, then, may not always be what they seem. Yet they are often more valuable than what we originally sought.

Thus, like the ancient Greeks, it is possible to reflect on tales of achievement and on overcoming the odds, which are stacked against a person. Tales of discovery and struggle are often couched in these terms. It is even the case that different struggles are combined into the same story. The 'mutiny' that Columbus suffered was probably borrowed from accounts of Bartholomew Diaz's expedition down the coast of Africa four years previously. Stories of struggle, then, usually draw on a variety of devices to ensure that the odds facing the protagonist are substantial and the prospects seem initially bleak.

These examples so far have involved a further theme, which is of therapeutic significance. That is, they reflect ideas about the image of a person, which other people have. This image may be partial and incomplete. Whereas most intellectuals by the time of Columbus were convinced the earth was spherical, this belief was not necessarily shared by the sailors, some of whom regarded Columbus as a madman who would sail them off the edge of the world. This theme of partial or tendentious perceptions is illustrated in many other stories, too, such as 'The elephant's parts' below:

THE ELEPHANT'S PARTS

There were six blind men who came across an elephant and tried to make out what they had found. The first man put his hands on the side of the elephant and declared he had found a wall. The second touched the trunk and said he had found a snake. The third man felt a tusk and claimed that he had found a spear. The fourth approached just as the elephant shook his large head and ears, and declared he had found a large fan. The fifth man came next as the elephant was passing water, and declared he had found a waterfall. The sixth had lost his footing and crawled under the elephant into something hot and sticky. 'You are all wrong,' he declared. 'It is toffee pudding and there's plenty for everyone,' and began to eat. They were all wrong based on what part of the elephant they encountered.

Similarities can be drawn from this on how we may be perceived. For example, in a similar way, often people 'get us wrong', depending on which part of us they see or experience. One person's judgement should not be taken as the truth about ourselves, whether the judgement is positive or negative. We are complex beings, with lots of parts to us. Sometimes we lose confidence when someone points out just one thing that is 'wrong with us', such as a large nose, a fat bum or aspects of our personality. We need to think of ourselves in terms of the elephant – we are always much more than any of our parts! The idea of icebergs being nine-tenths submerged comes to mind here. We can choose not to acquiesce to other people's limiting or narrow judgements of who we are.

This idea of human beings as consisting of many parts or many stories is an intriguing one from our point of view and is paralleled by a number of developments in the theory of the self in the latter part of the twentieth century. In accordance with this conviction that selves can be seen in important ways as sets of stories, a number of authors (MacIntyre, 1981; Sarbin, 1986a; Crossley, 2000) have put forward the idea that human psychology has a fundamentally narrative structure. For example, Sarbin proposes what he calls the 'narratory principle', which asserts that human beings think, perceive, imagine, interact and make moral choices according to narrative and story structures: 'A story is a symbolised account of actions of human beings that has a temporal dimension. The story has a beginning, middle, and an ending. ... The story is held together by recognisable patterns of events called plots. Central to the plot structure are human predicaments and attempted resolutions' (Sarbin, 1986b, p. 3).

Theodore Sarbin has for a number of years thought of narrative as the 'organising principle for human action'. The concept of narrative can be used to help account for the observation that human beings always seek to *impose structure* on the flow of experience. As Crossley (2000) notes, this narrative principle invokes a humanisitic image of the self as a teller of stories, of heroes and villains, plots, and images of actors performing and engaging in dialogue with other actors.

This kind of idea that the contemporary self is a mass of stories and a mosaic of meaningful experiences has been a central concern of other theorists too. In his book *The Saturated Self*, Kenneth Gergen (1991) portrays the 'dilemmas of identity in contemporary life':

> *Emerging technologies saturate us with the voices of humankind – both harmonious and alien. As we absorb their varied rhymes and reasons, they become part of us and we of them. Social saturation furnishes us with a multiplicity of incoherent and unrelated languages of the self. For everything we 'know to be true' about ourselves, other voices within respond with doubt and even derision. This fragmentation of self-conceptions corresponds to a multiplicity of incoherent and disconnected relationships. These relationships pull us in myriad directions, inviting us to play such a variety of roles that the very concept of an 'authentic self' with knowable characteristics recedes from view. The fully saturated self becomes no self at all.*

(pp. 6–7)

In this passage, Gergen emphasises the multiplicity, fragmentation and incoherence of the self in a postmodern world. We are, in a sense, a kind of bricolage or mosaic of different stories and experiences. Instead of having a 'one and only' authentic self, a new pattern of self consciousness is emerging. This is called by Gergen 'multiphrenia', the splitting of the individual into a multiplicity of self investments. For Gergen (1991), the state of multiphrenia is not a pathological one but 'is often suffused with a sense of expansiveness and adventure' (p. 74).

The adventure inherent in the exploration of new possibilities of selfhood is an important theme and one to which we shall return. Stories allow this variety and allow the imagination of possible worlds inhabited by different selves. They may also illustrate some of the techniques whereby these new selves can be achieved. They are, in the words of Michel Foucault, 'technologies of the self' in that they are a set series of techniques that allow individuals to work on themselves by regulating their bodies, their thoughts and their conduct.

A further important implication of Gergen's thinking in particular is that people are partly constituted through their relationships with others. These relationships may take a variety of forms and it is often through the modification of these that new possibilities of selfhood are opened up. Again, stories can provide a way of conceptualising and modifying the relationships within which the client is embedded. For example, Cascio and Gasker (2001) have developed Bram Stoker's *Dracula* story as a metaphor for destructive relationships. In the story one person's needs are met at the emotional and sexual expense of the other. The authors conceptualise the parasitic relationship.

> *A parasitic relationship includes one person who functions as the parasite and one who serves as the host. In such relationships, the emotional and/or sexual needs of one partner are met at the expense of the other person. The parasitic partner in such a relationship combats feelings of insecurity and inadequacy by being in control of the situation and the partner, at a terrible, life-draining cost to the partner. There is often an element of narcissism in the taking on of this parasitic role. Eventually, this robs the host partner of her or his self-esteem, feelings of efficacy in the environment, and the confidence to navigate everyday existence as a fully functioning individual. For some individuals being in a parasitic relationship confirms the self-image of a victim. For others, it is a seemingly imperceptible devolution into that role. This conceptualization of the parasitic relationship is purposely broad and meant to include a wide range of dysfunctional relationships, which can include co-dependent relationships, physically and/or emotionally abusive relationships, relationships characterized by infidelity, and by pairings which include marked emotional unavailability.*
>
> (pp. 20–1)

The authors identify five themes in such a relationship. First is *invitation*, meaning that the relationship is consensual. Second is *progression*, in terms of the 'seductive allure' of the vampire, resulting in a mixture of 'fear and desire' when attraction overrides rational thinking. Third is *inhumanity* whereby 'as the relationship develops, the participant's very personhood is lost. That is the Victim may adopt characteristics of her aggressor'. Fourth is *reversibility*, in the way that the struggle endured made the victim stronger, indicating that people can survive and go on to thrive after living through the destruction of a parasitic relationship. Finally, there is *termination* in that it is often not possible for someone to escape the throes of a parasitic relationship without help. The authors present a case study of them using this metaphor with a client. Cascio and Gasker (2001) also identify sub themes, so as to highlight, for example how *leaving* a destructive relationship is often more frightening than staying. Other sub themes include *multiple forms*, in that the Count assumes many forms like a parasitic partner, and being *unavailable emotionally*, such that 'The person uses the other in the relationship to satisfy his/her emotional and sexual needs but is unresponsive to him/herself in any meaningful way.'

If people are unfamiliar with the Dracula story then the basic themes can be retrieved from other stories with which the clients are familiar. Currently in the UK (and many other Western countries) soap operas are enormously popular and these provide a wealth of storylines. In the UK (2002/3) a storyline, which ran for some time in the popular BBC series *EastEnders*, featured an abusive relationship between two characters 'Little Mo' and 'Trevor'. This kind of plot, populated by familiar characters, may be more readily usable in therapeutic contexts. It demonstrates a process that is similar to the Dracula story. For instance, the relationship between the protagonists was initially consensual. Mo married Trevor freely, and frequently chose to go back to him following abuse. She loved him and was drawn to him, yet she feared him. The unfolding story showed how Trevor's inhumanity was leading her to lose sense of who she was. She became increasingly anxious and miserable as he prevented her from seeing her family and going out, and he became increasingly violent and sexually aggressive. Eventually, she adopted his tendencies and violently attacked him. The struggle she endured during and when leaving the relationship made her stronger and more assertive. We see her afterwards forming more positive and loving relationships. Also in terms of the sub themes she found leaving very hard, she doubted he would ever let her go and often felt it would be easier to accept the abuse. Trevor presented in many forms: sometimes he was caring and loving; sometimes vulnerable and needy. Yet he was unavailable emotionally and failed to respond to her needs such as wanting to have contact with her family of origin and requiring independence and support herself. In terminating the relationship the story showed her developing a kind of 'inner strength' and determination. At the same time she also needed help in the form of friends and family on the way to finally breaking free of him. After identifying the themes with clients, we can draw parallels between experiences of the characters and their own life. This process is aided by the fact that, in the UK especially, soap operas and TV series are often intended by their makers to have an educational function. Thus, when issues such as illness, rape or domestic violence are dealt with, the writers and producers may well take some trouble to base their stories on the knowledge gleaned by researchers and practitioners in the field. This was explicitly the case for Phil Redmond, who originated *Grange Hill* and *Brookside* with the deliberate intention of educating the viewers about social issues. Consequently, a knowledge of clients' viewing preferences and a working knowledge of the ongoing plotlines and characters can be an important way of helping people formulate their problems. This kind of approach might well help in exploratory work too. Simply saying 'If you were a character in a soap opera, who would you be?' might open up useful lines of enquiry. For those who are not soap fans, a character in a film or a novel can easily be substituted.

The Dracula story also illustrates how it is very easy to become entangled in interpersonal relationships in such a way that they become definitive of who we are. Whereas, according to many contemporary theories of the self, we are little more than the sum total of our social relationships and our stories, an overt dependency on the approval of others can yield a stultified and restricted approach to living. Once people confound others' admiration with their own self approval they may become extremely reliant on others to make them feel good. There are many circumstances where it might be desirable for clients to be less needy, clingy or reliant on others. As Ralph Waldo Emerson once said in his treatise on self reliance:

> To believe your own thought, to believe that what is true for you in your private heart is true for all men, – that is genius. Speak your latent conviction, and it shall be the universal sense; for the inmost in due time becomes the outmost, – and our first thought is rendered back to us by the trumpets of the Last Judgment. Familiar as the voice of the mind is to each, the highest merit we ascribe to Moses, Plato, and Milton is, that they set at naught books and traditions, and spoke not what men but what they thought. A man should learn to detect and watch that gleam of light which flashes across his mind from within, more than the lustre of the firmament of bards and sages.
>
> (Emerson, 1841)

The overall drift of this kind of thinking is to exhort the reader to greater and greater feats of independence and self reliance. The idea that habitual patterns of thinking help to create moods is of course a central tenet of cognitive and cognitive behavioural therapies. Here, it is believed that changing one's mood depends on changing one's patterns of thinking. As one of the most enthusiastic contemporary proponents of cognitive therapies, David Burns (1999, p. 28), puts it:

> Depression is not an emotional disorder at all! The sudden change in the way you feel is of no more causal relevance than a runny nose is when you have a cold. Every bad feeling you have is the result of your distorted negative thinking. Illogical pessimistic attitudes play the central role in the development and continuation of all your symptoms.

In this framework, it is believed that if a person firmly believes that they are bad or have let others down, they will tend to feel unmotivated to pursue their everyday activities. The less you do the easier it is to become preoccupied with unhelpful negative thoughts. If you do something, you will be temporarily distracted from that internal dialogue of self denigration. As Burns says: 'Almost all negative emotional reactions inflict their damage only as a result of low self-esteem. A poor self image is the magnifying glass that can transform a trivial mistake or an imperfection into an overwhelming symbol of personal defeat' (1999, p. 29).

Whereas the 'paralysis of will' characteristic of depression might prevent a person achieving anything useful or satisfying and thus deepening the depression, there is also the obverse problem of excessively driven achievement. A person may feel good about themselves only when they achieve something that they or others recognise. In some cases, their belief system motivates them to produce even more effort to achieve some degree of satisfaction. They are thus able to avoid the horrors of being 'just average'. However, there can be disadvantages to this kind of achievement motivation, such as when an individual becomes so preoccupied with worldly success that they become isolated from other potential sources of satisfaction and enjoyment. This happens when, for example, a person becomes a 'workaholic' and feels excessively driven to accomplish results. If they fail to keep up the pace, they will experience a sense of withdrawal characterised by inner emptiness and despair. In the absence of achievement they may feel worthless and bored without any other basis for self respect and fulfilment. This is the kind of dilemma faced by people who have worked hard for a number of years and are then incapacitated by illness or sudden redundancy. The difficulties of the person who is no longer able to work can readily lead to depression, on the understanding that since they are no longer producing they are no good.

This situation can be countered by the therapist in various ways. A story that one of the authors tells people who are having difficulties with this residual Protestant work ethic is about an acquaintance we have named 'the man who made litter'. The man was a chemical engineering graduate who got a job as a packaging chemist for a major snack food manufacturer. Diligently and with great resourcefulness he devised ever more cost effective ways of wrapping confectionery. His crowning moment came when he saw one of his newly designed wrappers in a hedge in Cornwall. What we see as achievements may well look trivial to others, or even, in this case, environmentally destructive. To take a more extreme case, Adolf Hitler clearly was a great achiever but did this make him particularly worthwhile? In cases like this, where a person is deprived of work, it is worth remembering the great philosopher and mathematician René Descartes, who famously stated '*Cogito ergo sum*' – I think therefore I am. He also famously said that if one wished to do good mathematics one should lie in bed in the mornings. Once, while lying in bed he followed the motions of a fly walking upside down on the ceiling and came to the conclusion that its position could be defined in relation to the edges of the room, thus leading to his system of Cartesian geometry with x, y and z axes, which has formed an important part of mathematics ever since. Great things can come of idleness as well as industry.

Importantly, then, this way of thinking abut human beings, their self image, their emotions and their sense of self worth relies on the kinds of stories, explanatory systems and values within which they are embedded. In this light, Kenneth Gergen postulates that Western culture is undergoing a fundamental change in the way it views the self as it begins to more fully acknowledge the influence of different stories on the self concept. Gergen believes that the thought structure of earlier psychology was heavily influenced by the romantic tradition. A human's true identity was believed to be contained in a deep, secretive and irrational inner world. This is reflected in nineteenth-century psychoanalytic notions where the forces driving human thinking and behaviour were largely hidden and could only be coaxed into view through the analysis of dreams, transference and mistakes or 'parapraxes'. Then, in the twentieth century, there was a period when psychology was very modernist, in which human beings were seen as special kinds of machines. According to modernistic thought, human behaviour can be measured scientifically, and is reliable and predictable. In this context, Gergen has been an important critic of trait models of personality and the idea that experimental results in psychology are reliable over time. Above all, Gergen's position is amenable to the idea that he regards the assumption that humans are determined through personal characteristics in various situations as the primary principle of an individualistic ideology, which scientists use to interpret the results of their research. According to Gergen, we are experiencing the end of the modernistic phase, and the postmodern phase is approaching. The postmodern phase involves a change in the way we think about science, art, society and the individual: 'the self as profound, as the bearer of characteristics such as commitment and strength of character, characteristics which are predictable and authentic, is coming under more and more criticism' (Gergen, 1990, p. 192).

Thus, as notions of the person as a self contained captain of his or her own ship become less widely accepted in the social sciences, the emphasis has increased on a model of the self, which is a kind of pot-pourri of fragments. This situation is favourable to our position in this book as it opens up the possibility that people can incorporate stories as part of their identity. This, as we shall see, may take a variety of forms and may be deployed by therapists to enrich, supplement or render a client's self more socially acceptable.

In this way, stories may be used to replace or supplement a part of the self that may be missing. This may, for example, be deployed in work with children with developmental disabilities. Del Valle et al. (2001) describe how very simple 'stories' may be used with autistic children so as to give them a sense of the consequences of some of their more disruptive or socially unusual behaviour. As they put it, a social story is a short story (i.e. two-to-five sentences) that describes a situation in terms of social cues and appropriate responses (Swaggart et al., 1995; Gray, 1998). These social stories serve a wide variety of purposes and can be adapted to suit the child's abilities and specific needs. Del Valle et al. (2001, p. 190) note that social stories can be used to: (a) introduce changes and new routines at home and school; (b) describe social situations and appropriate responses in a non-threatening way; (c) personalise or emphasise social skills; (d) explain and identify, in a realistic way, appropriate and inappropriate interactions depicted; and (e) teach academic lessons by relating learned skills to real situations (Gray, 1998; Heflin & Simpson, 1998).

Here are a couple of simple, instructive or non-imaginative stories presented by Del Valle et al. (2001):

Sometimes I bang my head on the wall.
When I bang my head it hurts.
If I keep banging my head I will get sick.
I don't want to get sick so I will stop banging my head.

(p. 191)

If I scream for what I want when I am in the store, when
I get home I will not be able to watch television that day.
If I ask for what I want quietly and do not scream,
I will get to watch television that day. I will also get ice cream.

(p. 194)

Thus children to whom these spare, factual-type stories are repeated may grasp more about the consequences of their actions and gain some insight into the workings of the more overt programmes of behaviour modification to which they may also be subject. In a sense, the ability to anticipate the future and to have a theory of mind, which may be very difficult for the autistic individual, can be supplemented by these simple narrativised instructions. What would be interesting, but to our knowledge has not been reported in the literature, would be to attempt this kind of thing with individuals suffering from emotional, cognitive or neurological impairments.

The use of stories, especially the more extended, imaginative kind, can also assist therapists seeking a non-threatening and non-stigmatising way of dealing with client's difficulties in developing an integrated sense of self. To illustrate this, let us consider a paper by Vaz (2001) entitled 'A woman in the grip of the archetype of the sexual priestess'. Despite the so called 'sexual revolution', there is still a core of thinking in the psychology of sexuality, which remains resolutely prescriptive and narrowly defines the appropriate behaviour of men and women. An interest in multiple partners and a preference for non-monogamous forms of relating to others will be taken by some theorists and therapists as signs of pathology and pejorative ideas such as 'sex addiction' may be deployed. In Vaz's description of her work with a client she describes how she was keen to avoid stigmatising her client through the use of addiction concepts or impose explanations on the sexual behaviour of the client, 'Natasha'. The client was already marginalised in terms of mainstream society's values. Vaz felt it would be unhelpful to replicate this 'othering' in the therapy of an individual whom mainstream society had so readily labelled anyway. 'Natasha' was a middle-aged mother and grandmother with a long history of involvement in the women's community. She maintained intimate relationships with past female lovers and with her ex-husband. In the years after her divorce, as Vaz describes the situation,

Natasha identified as a lesbian and engaged in neo-pagan goddess-based religions, practised sadomasochism in her lesbian relationships, and had a long-standing interest in communal living and polyamorous approaches to relationships. She socialised with friends of many years, but as she became more sexually attracted to men, she sought out acquaintances in the heterosexually oriented D/S (dominance/submission) community. Because her children deemed her heterosexual activities to be dangerous, their relationship with her was strained.

Some psychotherapists have tried to explore the meanings of the concept of goddesses of eroticism. Clarissa Pinkola Estes (1992) writes that there was a time when women's sexuality included the dimension of the sacred obscene; meaning sexually sapient and witty. Gleaning the stories of real and mythological women and dubbing them the 'dirty Goddess stories', Estes (1992) argued that these stories captured the ways women used sexuality to 'make a point, to lighten a sadness, to cause laughter, and in that way to set something aright that had gone wrong' (p. 335). She labelled them dirty since they came from the earth, the mud and muck of the psyche, which, in some mythological systems, are the prime material of creativity. This case also illustrates how it is possible to use stories and ideas from theological and mythological systems to successfully subvert the more oppressive features of conventional clinical wisdom too. Here, the client was assisted to a more comfortable appreciation of herself and empowered to make choices about the sorts of relationships she allowed herself to be drawn into. This occurred despite the apparent diversity and fragmentation of her life, which included elements that were both heterosexual and lesbian, and where she was a family member and a member of other intimate and political communities. The fragmentation noted by Gergen (1990) is survivable if we use the right stories.

In more mundane contexts it may also be possible to render an account of the importance of self acceptance and self nurturing. One form of this 'care of the self' narrative can be seen in terms of mechanical analogies. Putting petrol in a car can be argued to be like our work on ourselves to ensure our wellbeing. In a sense it needs topping up, just like us. Much as we monitor petrol, conserve it by not over-accelerating, by maintaining good tyre pressure and by not driving at high speed, so we need to conserve our own energies. Sometimes, if we overdo caring for others, and giving to others, this is rather like burning off all the petrol so that the car stops. Thus, we need to consider that as part of our self maintenance we may need to undertake a similar process of topping up or nurturing ourselves. This 'doing things for us' keeps our metaphorical car on the road. This kind of thinking has found its way into the English language in the form of similar phrases like 'recharge my batteries' or, in another electronic analogy, it is possible to speak of 'turning down the volume of the inner critic'.

Another piece of commonplace advice in contemporary self help literature is to give yourself credit for skills, abilities and recent achievements; to revisit aspects of past actions that are pleasing or satisfying. Even if past achievements are small, they are still an important part of nurturing oneself. Whereas this might seem mundane to us, there are some intriguing precedents for this in history. Ancient Greeks of the Homeric period saw in the ordinary stories of their lives the visible presence of gods, intervening from Mount Olympus. The Greek tragedies were a dramatic representation of how people saw their frail condition, but the everyday events of a person's life could be sacred too. The small successes were infused with the actions of the gods, just as much as great battles or heroic adventures.

Returning to the present day, it is perhaps worth thinking for a moment about some of the origins of the self concept in contemporary Western psychology. From developmental psychology we know that the concept of self starts to be constructed in infancy. Initially the infant is not able to see itself as separate from the mother but as it develops it is able to differentiate. During early infancy the child begins to form a view of itself in relation to the world that is influenced by the messages it receives. McMullin (2000) writes:

> As the self concept emerges, other aspects are gathered, including emotions. 'This thing called self is fearful, happy, hungry, or angry.' While the child is still at a young age, a very important thing takes place: the self starts gathering an overall value. Children start placing a positive or negative worth on this self ... [along the lines of]: 'This is a good self. This is a bad self. This is a flawed self. Others have better selves. This is an evil self. This self has merit. This self is worthless. This self is sick.'
>
> (p. 47)

Importantly, the child learns to view and value itself according to the feedback it gets from others. The valuation of the child by significant others in its life will be accepted uncritically or unquestioningly because the child's thinking is not sufficiently developed to contest or reinterpret this view of themselves.

Whatever the valuation of self by the child, related behaviours will tend to follow in its wake. In other words, as with a self fulfilling prophecy, a child who evaluates its 'self' as bad or incompetent, will tend to mirror this in bad or incompetent actions. Because of this confirming bias, these labels tend to remain fairly stable and influential throughout life.

Dimbleby and Burton (1998) provide a useful model for looking at the self. They divide self image into: 'the self as I believe I am'; 'the self I would like to be'; and 'the self as I believe others see me'. Briefly, the first of these consists of physical, intellectual and emotional images of the self. These self images, while they can be accurate, may not always tally with reality. For example, in anorexia, the individual may see themselves as fat, when, in fact, they are painfully thin. If individuals view themselves as unattractive it will affect how they communicate with others and thus lead to the rejection they anticipate. At the intellectual level, self image tends to be influenced by educational performance and the ability to be competent in language and hence communication. This competency reinforces notions of intellectual worth and promotes confidence and social action. People are often accurate at judging how they typically behave emotionally, however this emotional self image can be disproportionately influenced by key emotional events that happen to them and, if you like, set the benchmark for subsequent emotional responses. For example, the panic experienced by an individual at a football match, may lead them to panic at future matches and may even generalise to other situations where crowds are involved, such as busy shopping areas.

The second part of the model concerns 'the self as I would like to be'. Here, Dimbleby and Burton propose that individuals compare themselves to role models and try to live up to these. However, huge discrepancies can occur between the two, and then problems can arise for the individual. For example, a son may look up to the sporting success of his father but not have the same skills to achieve comparable results when competing. This may cause detrimental problems to the son's self esteem.

The third part of the model concerns the 'self as others see me'. Dimbleby and Burton point out that it is the feedback an individual gets from others that heavily influences their self image and self esteem. In relation to role theory, individuals tend to conform and behave according to a variety of role expectations that others and society have of them. Within the tradition of symbolic interactionism, as discussed by Mead (1934) and Goffman (1961), the notion of core selfhood is less compelling than that of selfhood being calibrated in response to the views of others. Of course, information about what others think of an individual will often be partial, since only some of these views will be communicated to that individual. Understandably, perhaps, individuals tend to seek out other people who support their view of themselves. Interestingly, the way that people narrate this often emphasises how they somehow knew they belonged to a particular group or had a certain kind of identity before this was fully revealed to them. Discovering the group was like discovering a part of themselves. Widdecombe and Woofitt's (1995) book on youth subcultures is replete with such accounts. In their own telling of their identity narrative, then, people are at pains to emphasise how they are autonomous agents and not just the pawns of 'peer pressure'. Hence, it might be difficult to persuade a client how apparently firmly entrenched parts of the self and identity may just as easily be thought of as coming from elsewhere. In Mick Inkpen's (1998) story *Nothing*, written for children, we find a useful structure for presenting to clients the way that our view of our selves [sic] is heavily governed by what others think of us. He writes:

> *A little, beat-up and discarded stuffed animal is left behind in the attic when a family moves. It is so old and ragged that its original form is no longer recognizable. It has been there so long that it has even forgotten its name. Even the movers left it behind. 'What have we got here?' said a voice. 'Oh, it's nothing,' said another. So the ragged little toy decides that* **Nothing** *must be its name.*

As George Herbert Mead put it: 'The self, as that which can be an object to itself, is essentially a social structure, and it arises out of social experience' (Mead, 1934, p. 140). The self looks like it is somehow inevitable and has always been present, but, in this view, it is profoundly social. Even earlier in the history of psychology William James had emphasised also the role of social relationships in creating the ideals against which we judge ourselves: '. . . the emotion that beckons me on is indubitably the pursuit of an ideal social self, a self that is at least worthy of approving recognition by the highest possible judging companion . . .' (James, 1910, p. 46).

As these quotes illustrate, the social nature of the self concept has long been appreciated. The quotes from Mead and James underscore the reciprocal perceptions of self and others as playing a crucial role in the self concept. Mead especially noted that we often form and manage our self images by interacting with others. Nearer the present time Murray (1989, p. 180) added to these formulations by suggesting that in doing this, individuals construct identities both by engaging in activity and by finding stories to tell about themselves. Indeed, in some cases lack of achievement in the actual activities can be compensated for by subsequent personal accounts of these activities, and the retrospective narrative has the attraction of fixing a meaning to one's actions, thus ensuring a certainty of interpretation. The idea of 'fisherman's tall stories' is a case in point here. The minuscule catch is contrasted with the size of the ones that were nearly landed but got away. Murray believes that the process of recounting self descriptions creates a sense of security for the self: 'Narrative enables the experiences of struggle and release to be inscribed in personal and collective memory' (Murray, 1989, p. 198).

The point being made here is that the person's identity is created rather than revealed through narrative. Whereas this point has by now been made by many theorists of the psychotherapeutic process, our contention in this volume is a little different. Our concern is how the stories can be made available to the individual so as to enable them to construct more effective, competent and even pleasurable identities.

Gergen, too, argues that the activity of self discourse creates, rather than relates, the 'self': 'mental talk is largely performative – that is, it does not mirror nor map an independent reality but is a functioning element in social process itself' (Gergen, 1989, p. 71). In this view, when we describe ourselves, we use the opportunity to reconstruct ourselves, in other words, to become what we describe. This challenges the assumption that the process of recounting experience and exchanging stories is a therapeutic by-product. Rather, taking these arguments seriously implies that when we communicate experience, content is judiciously selected and organised to satisfy the primary therapeutic purpose of self presentation. The stories at play in a therapy session may be those provided from the client's biography or imagination and those supplied by the therapist, or, sometimes, those they collaborate in producing. Harre (1989) describes how individuals often use metaphors of struggle to create an impression of an essential self. By deploying various biographical events and adopting an appropriate style they can offer 'the illusion of a transcendental ego'. Through employing a deterministic voice to present transformative experiences, people narrate their own stories so as to reinforce the conviction that an authentic self with an intrinsic individuality exists, and can be revealed and recovered. This narrated identity, while it may involve a common, enduring core, may nevertheless be talked about as if it has undergone transformations, which involve the substitution of new stories and identities. As one of the authors recently heard from a student, 'I used to be a right nutter but now I've calmed down'. The folly of one's youth is often contrasted with the rationality of the present.

Sometimes the grasping of a new self story can be momentous and result in a sense of sudden conversion. As Denzin (1989) claims in his account of biography and autobiography as research methods: 'The notion that lives are turned around by significant events, what I call epiphanies, is deeply entrenched in Western thought. At least since Augustine, the idea of transformation has been a central part of the autobiographical and biographical form' (1989, p. 23).

These 'significant events' are commonly deployed to illustrate and justify the narrator's development. The transformative nature of the incidents suggests progressive moral improvement, and this effect is further emphasised by the way the incidents are organised and presented. Take the following story, 'Choosing to live':

CHOOSING TO LIVE

Jerry is the kind of guy you love to hate. He is always in a good mood and always has something positive to say. When someone would ask him how he was doing, he would reply, 'If I were any better, I would be twins!'

He was a unique manager because he had several waiters who had followed him around from restaurant to restaurant. The reason the waiters followed Jerry was because of his attitude. He was a natural motivator. If an employee was having a bad day, Jerry was there telling the employee how to look on the positive side of the situation. Seeing this style really made me curious, so one day I went up to Jerry and asked him, 'I don't get it! You can't be a positive person all of the time. How do you do it?' Jerry replied, 'Each morning I wake up and say to myself, Jerry, you have two choices today. You can choose to be in a good mood or you can choose to be in a bad mood. I choose to be in a good mood.

'Each time something bad happens, I can choose to be a victim or I can choose to learn from it. I choose to learn from it. Every time someone comes to me complaining, I can choose to accept their complaining or I can point out the positive side of life. I choose the positive side of life.' 'Yeah, right, it's not that easy,' I protested. 'Yes it is,' Jerry said. 'Life is all about choices. When you cut away all the junk, every situation is a choice. You choose how you react to situations. You choose how people will affect your mood. You choose to be in a good mood or bad mood. The bottom line: It's your choice how you live life.'

I reflected on what Jerry said. Soon thereafter, I left the restaurant industry to start my own business. We lost touch, but I often thought about him when I made a choice about life instead of reacting to it. Several years later, I heard that Jerry did something you are never supposed to do in a restaurant business: he left the back door open one morning and was held up at gunpoint by three armed robbers. While trying to open the safe, his hand, shaking from nervousness, slipped off the combination. The robbers panicked and shot him. Luckily, Jerry was found relatively quickly and rushed to the local trauma center.

111

After 18 hours of surgery and weeks of intensive care, Jerry was released from the hospital with fragments of the bullets still in his body.

I saw Jerry about six months after the accident. When I asked him how he was, he replied, 'If I were any better, I'd be twins. Wanna see my scars?'

I declined to see his wounds, but did ask him what had gone through his mind as the robbery took place. 'The first thing that went through my mind was that I should have locked the back door' Jerry replied. 'Then, as I lay on the floor, I remembered that I had two choices: I could choose to live or I could choose to die. I chose to live.' 'Weren't you scared? Did you lose consciousness?' I asked. Jerry continued, '. . . the paramedics were great. They kept telling me I was going to be fine. But when they wheeled me into the ER and I saw the expressions on the faces of the doctors and nurses, I got really scared. In their eyes, I read "he's a dead man". I knew I needed to take action.' 'What did you do?' I asked. 'Well, there was a big burly nurse shouting questions at me,' said Jerry. 'She asked if I was allergic to anything. "Yes" I replied. The doctors and nurses stopped working as they waited for my reply. I took a deep breath and yelled, "Bullets!" Over their laughter, I told them, "I am choosing to live. Operate on me as if I am alive, not dead."'

(Adapted from story by Brian Cavanaugh 1997–99 Cyber Quotations)

Whereas this story has described momentous and life threatening events, there are other kinds of anecdote, which emphasise the creation of equanimity in the face of more quotidian events. Many people find themselves in difficult, boring or unrewarding jobs. The following story, 'The trouble tree', is useful when suggesting to clients changes in the way they express themselves outside of work. Often, we take our work problems home to the extent that the 'self' we are at home resembles the 'self' loaded up with various troubles or problems at work. The metaphor of the 'trouble tree' reminds us that we can choose to offload the 'work self' and allow a less troubled, more relaxed 'home self' to emerge.

THE TROUBLE TREE

The carpenter I hired to help me restore an old farmhouse had just finished a rough first day on the job. A flat tire made him lose an hour of work, his electric saw quit, and now his ancient pickup truck refused to start.

While I drove him home, he sat in stony silence. On arriving, he invited me in to meet his family. As we walked toward the front door, he paused briefly at a small tree, touching tips of the branches with both hands. When opening the door, he underwent an amazing transformation. His tanned face was wreathed in smiles and he hugged his two small children and gave his wife a kiss.

Afterward he walked me to the car. We passed the tree and my curiosity got the better of me. I asked him about what I had seen him do earlier. 'Oh, that's my trouble tree,' he replied. 'I know I can't help having troubles on the job, but one thing's for sure, troubles don't belong in the house with my wife and the children. So I just hang them up on the tree every night when I come home. Then in the morning I pick them up again.

'Funny thing is,' he smiled, 'when I come out in the morning to pick 'em up, there ain't nearly as many as I remember hanging up the night before.'

(Author unknown)

A similar story about preserving a self despite the potentially negative influence of work environments is 'A place to stand' by Charles Garfield, which depicts well how we can begin to preserve aspects of self that can be lost in many work environments and how we might be able to find new solutions within various social constraints or circumstances we find ourselves in.

A PLACE TO STAND

If you have ever gone through a toll booth, you know that your relationship to the person in the booth is not the most intimate you'll ever have. It is one of life's frequent non-encounters: You hand over some money; you might get change; you drive off. Late one morning in 1984, headed for lunch in San Francisco, I drove toward a booth. I heard loud music. It sounded like a party. I looked around. No other cars with their windows open. No sound trucks. I looked at the toll booth. Inside it, the man was dancing.

'What are you doing?' I asked.

'I'm having a party,' he said.

'What about the rest of the people?' I looked at the other toll booths.

He said, 'What do those look like to you?' He pointed down the row of toll booths.

'They look like ... toll booths. What do they look like to you?'

He said, 'Vertical coffins. At 8:30 every morning, live people get in. Then they die for eight hours. At 4:30, like Lazarus from the dead, they reemerge and go home. For eight hours, brain is on hold, dead on the job. Going through the motions.'

I was amazed. This guy had developed a philosophy, a mythology about his job. Sixteen people dead on the job, and the seventeenth, in precisely the same situation, figures out a way to live. I could not help asking the next question: 'Why is it different for you? You're having a good time.'

He looked at me. 'I knew you were going to ask that. I don't understand why anybody would think my job is boring. I have a corner office, glass on all sides. I can see the Golden Gate, San Francisco, and the Berkeley hills. Half the Western world vacations here . . . and I just stroll in every day and practice dancing.'

(Cited in Cyber Quotations 1997–9)

Whether we are looking at self development in or around the work environment or elsewhere, it is vital that people make time for themselves, for their needs as individuals. Our lives are often so filled with work and chores that we fail to do the things that give us the most meaning and pleasure, which are often the simple things like spending time with our partner or taking a leisurely walk around the block. We prioritise elsewhere in taking up a variety of demanding and sometimes competing roles – whether as mother, father, teacher, student and so on – but these aren't always the things that enrich us. We need to balance time and prioritise a good portion of it for ourselves because so often what you want to be is the first thing to go as you race to fulfil other people's demands.

TIME FOR YOU

Imagine owning a bank account which is credited every new day with £86,400, carries over no balance from day to day, allows you to keep no cash balance, and every evening cancels whatever part of the amount you had failed to use during the day. What would you do? Draw out every penny, of course! Well, everyone has such a bank. Its name is TIME. Every morning, it credits you with 86,400 seconds. Every night it writes off, as lost, whatever of this you have failed to invest to good purpose. It carries over no balance. It allows no overdraft.

Each day it opens a new account for you. Each night it burns the records of the day. If you fail to use the day's deposits, the loss is yours. There is no going back. There is no drawing against the 'tomorrow'. You must live in the present on today's deposits. But how much of this time credit do you use for 'you' – that is, time set aside everyday to refresh and restore your 'self'?

(adapted from Author Unknown)

There are many stories that emphasise self survival, the need to take opportunities to preserve who we are and take steps to negotiate this rather than get exhausted by fighting against the various ways that society and other people can try to shape us and make us into something we are not. There is no easy process in preserving core aspects of who we are or becoming who we want to be, however multiphrenic. Sometimes our circumstances call for careful handling, and achieving what we want for ourselves in the best way possible. The following, adapted from Burns (1999), illustrates this well:

GOING WITH THE FLOW

A boy and his father go fishing in a boat on a river. They take the family dog, Churchill, who loves the water and tends to stand with his paws on the prow of the boat watching for the fish that would occasionally break the surface. Unfortunately, Churchill got rather excited as the young boy landed a large fish and fell into the water. The current quickly pulled him away from the boat and the young boy panicked as the dog swan downstream instead of back to the boat. The boy screamed for the dog to swim back to the boat, but the father told him to let Churchill find his own way: 'If he tries to swim against the current he will quickly tire and even if he reached the boat the sides would make it difficult to pull him on board. Relax, he knows what to do.' But the boy watched anxiously as the dog he loved moved further and further downstream. 'Learn from him,' the father said. 'Don't fight against a force that is stronger than you. Go with it and use it. Churchill is letting the current take him, while gradually making his way to the bank.' The father then turned the boat around and followed Churchill downstream. Eventually, they caught sight of him on the far bank barking cheerfully and wagging his tail. 'See,' said the father. 'He went with the flow and used it to his advantage.'

Sometimes it's not who we are but how we sell ourselves that is the important issue. Barker (1996) describes the development of two competing video cassette systems – BETA and VHS:

> *Before it was clear which system would prevail in the marketplace, I sought the advice of several experts in the field. Their unanimous opinion was that the BETA system was the better of the two. Despite this, it was the VHS system that gained popularity at the expense of the BETA system. VHS became standard for home use and nowadays it is hard to find a BETA tape in most video rental stores or to buy a video cassette recorder for use at home – though I understand that the BETA system is still quite widely used in industry. It seemed that the better system failed to become the standard for domestic use. How could this have come to pass? The fact seems to be that 'It is not what you are selling but how you are selling it.'*

In the light of this, it might be possible to draw some parallels between the technical merits of different kinds of video systems and the self. In a sense, the self is a product or brand. It has a demographic segment to which it can be marketed and the advertising campaign can advantageously be developed so as to present the self in the most favourable light. Selves that are perfectly good but have a lacklustre advertising campaign may not do as well as ones that may be less appealing but are marketed more aggressively. Once we have acknowledged our unique selling points and our value added aspects it is important to consider how to present them most effectively.

This issue of presenting oneself effectively to others is particularly important in the light of the renewed emphasis in social psychology on this interpersonal nature of the self concept. If our selves are marketed effectively then it is more likely that we would gain the kinds of support, acceptance and social integration that we desire. Baumeister and Leary (1995) contend that the desire to belong and be accepted by others is the strongest, most central human motivation. Research in a variety of fields, such as on attachment theory, interpersonal relationships (Murray & Holmes, 1993; Holmes, 2000), and culture (Lee et al., 2000), has underscored the role of other people in helping to create the individual's self concept. Because the self concept is informed by these self/other perceptions, concerns that this interpersonal aspect of the self can be particularly threatening to individuals, particularly in individualistic Western cultures. Since William James's generative work, the literature on the self concept has yielded many examples of how the self responds in defensive, biased ways to try to protect itself against such threats.

Spencer et al. (2001) provide further support for the idea that interpersonal dynamics play a pivotal role in the self concept. The potential failure of interpersonal processes can trigger self protective motivations and provide the mechanisms through which individuals try to satisfy this motivation, such as through self presentation or social comparison routes. When people think about an important value, however, they appear to feel less vulnerable to interpersonal threats and are less likely to resort to these routes to restore their self image. It is at points like this that stories encapsulating the issues that an individual finds important can be vital in sustaining wellbeing. Fein and Spencer (1997) suggested that people can use their perceptions of themselves *vis-à-vis* others to cope with other threats to their self image, and later (Spencer et al., 2001) they identified how the relationship can go the other way too, in that people can draw on other aspects of their self-image to cope with threats to their self *vis-à-vis* others. The loss of others' approval is sustainable if we believe that some greater value has been served. Losing the approval of one's crew is sustainable if we believe the treasures of the orient are just over the horizon.

One way of ensuring that we or our clients have some sort of reserve of energy to help us over the temporary blips in the matrix of social relationships is to ensure that we are informed by a diversity of sustaining stories. In other words, whereas we might be a mosaic of different stories, images and ideas, it is possible to ensure that there is a sufficient variety of these at hand to enable us to cope with whatever circumstances present themselves. The concept of 'social saturation' identified by Gergen is supposedly the 'occupation of the self' with the values and lifestyles of others. Because of our multiple encounters:

> '... we absorb others into ourselves so to speak: we take individual parts of their lives with us. ... Each of us is becoming more and more a colourful mixture of potentials, whereby each potential represents one or more relationships in which we are involved. ... If individuals are the result of relationships, one must conclude that relationships are more basic than individuals.'

> (Gergen, 1990, pp. 195, 197)

Yet at the same time it is important to be aware of what individuals do with the culturally available materials from which they construct their identities. With all the preceding ideas in mind, the constitutive role of language, culture and social relations in the formation of self is undeniable. Indeed, it makes good sense to speak of the social constitution of the self. But the word *construction* implies something quite different. It implies a building process, an act of labour, design and transformation. 'Something created', Bakhtin (1986) writes, 'is always created out of something given. What is given', he is quick to add, 'is completely transformed in what is created' (p. 120). Hence, according to this tradition, there is a good deal of support for the notion that people incorporate stories and somehow make them their own in constructing an identity through an active process of negotiating meanings and assigning order to specific life circumstances. Nevertheless, as some authors have pointed out (McLeod, 1997; Androutso-poulou, 2001), we actually know very little about *how* the incorporation of stories helps people with problems around emotions or identity. Examining popular self help literature and its audience, McLeod (1997) has questioned whether the direct advice found in these self help guides has any effectiveness at all, even when these are read in conjunction with psychotherapy. Cohen (1994) noted that according to clients' reports, clients benefited most by entering into the stories of people recounted in the book, rather than by reading any other sections. It is the stories of people in similarly difficult circumstances in other words that are believed to be the most effective parts of the book.

In one sense it is as if the stories of other people and their misfortunes are concrete and lifelike for the readers, yet in another way they are profoundly metaphorical. Paul Ricoeur's reflections on metaphor may be useful in this context. The 'metaphorical process', as he put it (1981), may be understood in terms of 'resemblance'. As such, a metaphor proclaims that *this* is akin to *that*. At the same time, however, Ricoeur emphasises, it is essential to recognise that the process at hand is a constructive one; it is a *making similar*, involving what he calls *predicative assimilation*, a sort of imaginative labour, which provides new ways of reading and describing the self. That is, the reader has to work hard to produce the resemblances themselves between a story and thus in reading popular self help literature, one has to work hard to create the resemblance between oneself and a 'woman who loves too much' in Robin Norwood's famous formulation, or a 'sex addict' or see oneself as a 'Mars' or 'Venus' in John Gray's popular relationship series. Thus, following Ricouer, we can speak of the *production* of resemblance – 'this is akin to that'; 'I am like the person in the story' – only to the extent that we can actively create such an affinity and bring together what might otherwise seem like very different accounts and experiences. This very act of positing affinity emerges, again, in and through the semantic potential of language itself. 'The difficulty', therefore, 'is to understand that we see similarity by construing it, that the visionary grasping of resemblance is, at the same time, a verbal invention. ... This is why the most effective analysis of metaphor concerns the construction which accompanies the vision'. It is also why these acts of meaning and imagination are best conceptualised in terms of 'the discursive and not the intuitive process involved in the creation of meaning' (Ricoeur, 1991a, p. 79). Rather than 'the faculty of deriving "images" from sensory experience', it is 'the capacity to let new worlds build our self-understanding' (Ricoeur, 1991b, p. 318).

As Wollheim (1984) pointed out, the sort of activity being considered here is to be understood as a *practical* activity: 'In reconstructing his [or her] development, a person reactivates it. In this way there is a tendency to move from self-interpretation to self-assessment, from self-assessment to self-criticism, from self-criticism to self-change' (p. 187).

As Gergen has noted in *The Saturated Self* (1991), 'much of our contemporary vocabulary of the person . . . finds its origins in the romantic period. It is a vocabulary of passion, purpose, depth, and personal significance: a vocabulary that generates awe of heroes, of genius, and of inspired work' (p. 27). Now, on some level, of course, speaking of the human condition in terms of stories, parables and anecdotes as Freeman (1999) notes, brings into play a somewhat romantic vocabulary, perhaps taking its cue from poets, many of whom are more than willing still to speak of passion, purpose, depth and personal significance. This then is one of the legacies of using stories. Whereas once upon a time these kinds of qualities were the terms in which the human condition was described, the last hundred years of psychology has introduced a good deal of scepticism about them. The present day academic vocabulary is not nearly so romantic or appealing, no matter whether the person is seen as being filled with personality traits or as a postmodern nomad appropriating cultural bric-à-brac. However, it is through stories that we can make ourselves more fully human, experience something of the consciousness of others and call to mind the commendable qualities we value. Through parable and metaphor we can, like the ancient Greeks, infuse ourselves and others with the armour of the gods. For as David Lodge notes in his recent book, *Consciousness and the Novel*, 'literature', which includes short and long prose and poetry, 'is a record of human consciousness, the richest and most comprehensive we have' (2002, p. 10).

REFERENCES

Androutsopoulou, A. (2001) Fiction as an aid to therapy: A narrative and family rationale for practice. *Journal of Family Therapy*, **23**, 278–95.

Bakhtin, M. M. (1986) *Speech genres and other late essays*. Austin, Tex.: University of Texas Press.

Barker, P. (1996) *Psychotherapeutic metaphors: A guide to theory and practice*. New York: Brunner/Mazel.

Baumeister, R. F & Leary, M. R. (1995) The need to belong: Desire for interpersonal attachments as a fundamental human motivation. *Psychological Bulletin*, **117**, 497–529.

Burns, D. D. (1999) *Feeling good*. New York: Wholecare Books.

Cascio, T. & Gasker, J. (2001) The vampire's seduction: Using Bram Stoker's Dracula as a metaphor in treating parasitic relationships. *Journal of Poetry Therapy*, **15**(1), 19–28.

Cohen, L. J. (1994) Bibliotherapy: a valid treatment modality. *Journal of Psychosocial Nursing*, **32**(9), 40–4.

Crossley, M. (2000) Narrative psychology, trauma and the study of self/identity. *Theory and Psychology*, **10**(4), 527–46.
http://www.cyberquotations.com/stories/adrift.htm.

Del Valle, P. R., McEachern, A. G. & Chambers, H. D. (2001) Using social stories with autistic children. *Journal of Poetry Therapy*, **14**(4), 187–97.

Denzin, N. (1989) *Interpretative biography*. London: Sage.

Dimbleby, R. & Burton, G. (1998) *More than words: An introduction to communication* (3rd edn). London: Routledge.

Emerson, R. W. (1841) Self reliance, In Essays, first series, reprinted on RWE.org – The works of Ralph Waldo Emerson, *http://rwe.org/works/Essays-1st_Series_02_Self-Reliance.htm*, (accessed 1/6/2003)

Estes, C. P. (1992) *Women who run with the wolves: Myths and stories of the wild woman archetype*. New York: Ballantine Books.

Fein, S. & Spencer, S. J. (1997) Prejudice as self-image maintenance: Affirming the self through negative evaluations of others. *Journal of Personality and Social Psychology*, 73, 31–44.

Foucault, M. (1986) *The care of the self*. New York: Pantheon Books.

Foucault, M. (1997) Technologies of the self. In P. Rabinow (Ed.). *Ethics: Subjectivity and truth* (translated by R. J. Hurley). New York: New Press.

Freeman, M. (1999) Culture, narrative and the poetic construction of selfhood. *Journal of Constructivist Psychology*, 12, 99–116.

Gergen, K. J. (1989) Warranting voice and the elaboration of the self. In J. Shotter & K. J. Gergen (Eds.). *Texts of identity*. London: Sage.

Gergen, K. J. (1990) *The saturated self: Dilemmas of identity in contemporary life*. New York: Basic Books.

Gergen, K. J. (1999) *An invitation to social construction*. London: Sage.

Goffman, E. (1961) *The presentation of self in everyday life*. New York: Doubleday.

Gray, D. E. (1998) *Autism and the family: Problems, prospects, and coping with the disorder*. Springfield, Ill.: Charles C. Thomas.

Harre, R. (1989) Language games and the texts of identity. In J. Shotter & K. J. Gergen (Eds.). *Texts of identity*. London: Sage.

Heflin, L. & Simpson, R. (1998) Interventions for children and youth with autism: Prudent choices in a world of exaggerated claims and empty promises. *Focus on Autism and Other Developmental Disabilities*, 13(4), 194–211.

Holmes, J. G. (2000) Social relationships: The nature and function of relational schemas. *European Journal of Social Psychology*, 30, 447–95.

Inkpen, M. (1998) *Nothing*. New York: Orchard Books.

James, W. (1910) *Psychology: The briefer course*. New York: Henry Holt.

Kurman, J., Yoshihara-Tanaka, C. & Elkoshi, T. (2003) Is self-enhancement negatively related to constructive self-criticism? Self-enhancement and self-criticism in Israel and in Japan. *Journal of Cross-Cultural Psychology*, 34(1), 24–37.

Lee, A. Y., Aaker, J. L. & Gardner, W. L. (2000) The pleasures and pains of distinct self-construals: The role of interdependence in regulatory focus. *Journal of Personality and Social Psychology*, 78, 1122–34.

Lodge, D. (2002) *Consciousness and the novel*. London: Secker & Warburg.

MacIntyre, A. (1981) *After virtue*. Notre Dame, NY: Notre Dame University Press.

McLeod, J. (1997) *Narrative and Psychotherapy*. London: Sage.

McMullin, R. E. (2000) *Handbook of cognitive therapy techniques*. New York: W. W. Norton.

Mead, G. H. (1934) *Mind, self, and society*. Chicago: University of Chicago Press.

Murray, K. (1989) The construction of identity in the narratives of romance and comedy. In J. Shotter & K. J. Gergen (Eds.). *Texts of identity*. London: Sage.

Murray, S. & Holmes, J. G. (1993) Seeing virtues in faults: Negativity and the transformation of interpersonal narratives in close relationships. *Journal of Personality and Social Psychology*, 65, 707–22.

Otto, M. W. (2000) Stories and metaphors in cognitive behavior therapy. *Cognitive and Behavioural Practice*, 7, 166–72.

Ricoeur, P. (1981) The metaphorical process as imagination, cognition, and feeling. In M. Johnson (Ed.). *Philosophical perspectives on metaphor*. Minneapolis, Minn.: University of Minnesota Press.

Ricoeur, P. (1991a) Word, polysemy, metaphor: Creativity in language. In M. J. Valdes (Ed.). *A Ricoeur reader*. Toronto, Canada: University of Toronto Press.

Ricoeur, P. (1991b) Metaphor and the main problem of hermeneutics. In M. J. Valdes (Ed.). *A Ricoeur reader*. Toronto, Canada: University of Toronto Press.

Sarbin, T. R. (Ed.)(1986a) *Narrative psychology: The storied nature of human conduct*. New York: Praeger.

Sarbin, T. R. (1986b) The narrative as a root metaphor for psychology, In T. R. Sarbin (Ed.). *Narrative psychology: The storied nature of human conduct*. New York: Praeger.

Shay, J. (1994) *Achilles in Vietnam: Combat trauma and the undoing of character*. New York: Athaneum.

Spencer, S. J., Fein, S. & Lomore, C. D. (2001) Maintaining one's self-image vis-a-vis others: The role of self-affirmation in the social evaluation of the self. *Motivation and Emotion*, **25**(1), 41–65.

Swaggart, B., Gagnon, E., Bock, S., Earles, T., Quinn, C., Myles, B., & Simpson, L. (1995) Using social stories to teach social and behavioral skills to children with autism. *Focus On Autistic Behavior*, **10**(1), 1–15.

Vaz, K. M. (2001) A woman in the grip of the archetype of the sexual priestess. *The Arts in Psychotherapy*, **28**, 57–69.

Widdecombe, S. & Wooffitt, R. (1995) *The language of youth subcultures*. London: Routledge.

Wollheim, R. (1984) *The thread of life*. Cambridge, Mass.: Harvard University Press.

Afterword

In this brief concluding section we will reflect on the issues that have been raised so far in the book and attempt to develop the implications of these for the reader. The aim is not to make any definitive statements about the nature of storytelling in therapy but instead to give readers a little 'escape velocity' so that they are aware of some of the possibilities and may be encouraged to take them seriously in their own practice, if they are therapists. Even for the lay person it is important to be aware of the power of stories to transform their lives and those of others around them.

Seeing psychotherapy partly as a process of giving and receiving stories aligns it with some very venerable traditions indeed. Healing arts and rituals, as well as popular culture itself, have often involved this sort of process. In the British Isles the bardic tradition has played an important role in the culture and it is appropriate to reflect on this for a moment. The term 'bard', in Wales, denoted a master-poet; while in Ireland it meant a poet who was not of the highest rank and perhaps had not undertaken all the formal training. But such was the importance of poetry and storytelling in Celtic cultures, the bard was pretty much a sacred person. He (and it usually was a 'he') could travel anywhere, say anything, and perform when and where he pleased. The bard was the bearer of news and the carrier of messages, and, if he was harmed, then nobody found out what was happening in the next village. In addition, he carried the custom of the country as memorised verses. He could be consulted in cases of customary or common law. He was, therefore, a valuable repository of cultural information, wisdom and news, as well as entertainment (Graves, 1966; Frazer, 1900). This role of course is not identical to psychotherapy. However, there are elements of the craft of the storyteller, which are similar between folklore and psychotherapeutic traditions. Like Bardic stories, those used in therapy do not need to be static. They can be revised and rewritten constantly so as to suit the circumstances and the audience involved.

There has been a great deal of attention devoted so far in the literature to clients themselves as storytellers but the kinds of stories that might be told by therapists have remained almost invisible. Yet personal experience tells us that most therapists have anecdotes they might use and re-use with clients, favourite ways of explaining things or even techniques of delivery that seem to work well in therapeutic encounters.

Within psychology the importance of stories and anecdotes has only recently been appreciated. Yet it is by attending to the story-like qualities of what we say that we make it convincing, resonant and compelling. Facts very rarely speak for themselves. It is the storyteller who is, in a sense, the ventriloquist.

Psychotherapy has a long history of being informed by learning theories. The treatment of anxiety disorders, for example, was revolutionised by the widespread adoption of behaviour therapies as a result of their enthusiastic promoter Joseph Wolpe (Wolpe et al., 1962). It was rather later that Mahoney and Thoresen provided their analyses of the role of verbal representations in behaviour acquisition and change, and demonstrated the limitations of 'cognition-free' behaviourism. Their seminal book, *Self control: Power to the person*, heralded the contemporary age of cognitively oriented therapies, which opened up a space in which theorists and therapists could begin to think about the therapeutic work that was done by the stories.

If we were to take the idea of stories and the people they inspire to its conclusion we might draw the reader's attention to Chadwick's (2001) *Personality as art*, where, as the title suggests, the individual's personality is seen as a kind of creative art form. In Chadwick's view, through devices such as music, poetry and artistic expression, the person can be seen in terms of beauty and self expression rather than in terms merely of structure and function or as a cluster of attitudinal or cognitive variables.

A further issue worth exploring is how therapists can become story collectors and story authors in their own right. Part of the art of becoming a story creator is being able to use oneself as a resource. Subject to the appropriate use of self disclosure, our own experiences can provide the raw material for anecdotes, but perhaps more importantly, it is worth attending to our feelings as we hear stories or reminisce about our own experiences. The chances are that if we find a story sad or uplifting it will have a similar effect on others too. In creating stories it is important to be aware of and utilise these intuitions. Manuals of writing often give this process rather florid titles such as 'writing with our hearts', 'writing down the bones', 'writing with the barest essence of ourselves' or 'taking dictation from the muse'. Those with a more psychodynamic bent might see it as following our 'subconscious'. More specifically, story creation is at its best when we are not initially worrying about impressing our potential listeners, editors or colleagues, or dazzling friends with our brilliance. The idea is that when we write or speak for and from ourselves, we are not only more productive but we are also making better use of our own intuitions about the story and thus produce one that might make contact with others more readily. People who teach writing say that the best way to learn how to do this is to sit and write as much as one can in a limited amount of time and try to suspend the internal censor. This is similar to the process of brainstorming where ideas are generated as rapidly, and with as little evaluation, as possible. The process of refinement can be undertaken later.

It is difficult in developing a therapeutic regime such as we are advocating to provide precise guidelines or a treatment manual. To set up rules and specific guidelines like this assumes that we know what the client will do, and this involves assuming that the knower need not be there to interact with what is out there in the client. Perhaps it is advisable to take a leaf out of the book of those who style themselves 'constructive therapists', and listen in good faith and hear what the knower can tell us of his or her personal reality and experience and tailor our storytelling accordingly. In telling stories, we cannot easily know what the client is experiencing, or that this is what other learners in the past have experienced.

Paulo Freire (1985) said that when the revolutionary begins to assume that he knows what is best for the members of the revolution, he has ceased to be a revolutionary. Likewise, when the storyteller begins to assume what the hearer 'knows' and is feeling about that learning, without the active participation of the learner, he or she has ceased to be an educator or therapist. We cannot write the rule books without assuming that we can 'know' what the learner knows. Thus storytelling must remain a flexible and spontaneous approach that can be a potent ally in teaching and healing others.

REFERENCES

Chadwick, P. K. (2001) *Personality as art*. Ross-on-Wye: PCCS Books.

Frazer, J. G. (1900) *The golden bough: A study in magic and religion*. London: Macmillan & Co.

Freire, P. (1985) *Pedagogy of the oppressed*. Harmondsworth: Penguin.

Graves, R. (1966) *The white goddess*. New York: Farrar, Straus & Giroux.

Mahoney, M. J. & Thoresen, C. E. (1974) *Self control: power to the person*. Monterey, Calif.: Brooks Cole.

Wolpe, J., Salter, A. & Reyna, L. J. (1962) *The conditioning therapies. The challenge in psychotherapy*. New York: Holt, Rinehart & Winston.

Index